SMALL GROUP MINISTRY

SMALL GROUP MINISTRY
in the Contemporary Church

By T. Ed Barlow

Copyright © 1972
HERALD PUBLISHING HOUSE
Independence, Missouri

Library of Congress Catalog Card No. 72-90357
ISBN-0-8309-0080-2

Printed in the United States of America

This book is dedicated to the Saints in Oklahoma. I am deeply grateful for the Christian love my family found during two missionary assignments in the Tulsa and Oklahoma City districts where the experiences and ideas for this book evolved.

"Appoint among yourselves a teacher, and let not all be spokesmen at once, but let one speak at a time, and let all listen to his sayings, that when all have spoken, that all may be edified of all, and that every man may have an equal privilege."

—Doctrine and Covenants 85:37b.

CONTENTS

PREFACE

For a long time I have felt a restless concern for more effective ways to communicate the faith of the Restoration Church to more people. The gospel of Jesus Christ is the answer to modern man's deepest needs yet many local churches seem so ineffective at getting this across. My search for a better approach led to experimentation. My interest in the small group approach was quickened in 1961 when a friend, Leonard Clark, gave me a copy of Samuel Shoemaker's book, *An Experiment of Faith*. An introduction to Shoemaker opened up a new world for me. He was the spiritual father of Alcoholics Anonymous, a prolific writer, an exponent of personal witnessing, and the founder of Faith at Work. I read every book he wrote and had the privilege of corresponding with him briefly before his death. While we never met, I owe a great debt to Dr. Sam. He introduced me to small groups, a vital solution to the contemporary church's need.

At a Faith at Work Conference in Kansas City I met Keith Miller, Ben Johnson, Bruce Larson, and a number of stimulating leaders who utilize the small group in personal ministry. They confirmed my growing convictions regarding the value of small groups in local churches.

Paul Tournier, O. H. Mower, John Drakeford, Sidney Jouard, and John Casteel are only a few who further contributed to my conviction that the small group is an effective method for contemporary congregational life. Elton Trueblood and Frank Buckman advocated small groups for several years and were two of the initial modern leaders to see their value.

Graduate course work at Tulsa University exposed me to Kurt Lewin, Carl Rogers, and other experts in the field of group dynamics. Chapter 13 in this book is a condensed report of the pilot project on attitude change in small groups conducted at Tulsa University to complete requirements for an advanced degree in counseling.

Earl Harder, Tulsa District president at that particular time, and Jack Basse, the present self-sustaining stake missionary, were co-workers in our first experiments with small group ministry. Many devoted priesthood men and women in Oklahoma worked with me, and we learned as we failed and evaluated. We have seen lives changed, new converts won, and church relationships deepened in many small groups over the past decade.

The attitude today is vastly different than ten years ago when small groups were first being reintroduced to the church. I am grateful for such men in the church as Dr. Charles Mader of the University of Illinois, Dr. Howard Clark of Texas Wesleyan University, Dr. Raymond Troyer of Southern Illinois University, and Gerald Gabriel of the University of Missouri—all self-sustaining ministers who have helped to encourage small groups in the church. These are only a few. Apostle Charles Neff and the missionaries in the Orient were early proponents of small groups.

Chapter 12 is a survey of current leadership opinions regarding small groups. The mood is quickly shifting toward this contemporary type of ministry in congregational life.

A recent development of the basic small group idea is called "house churches." Several congregations in Oklahoma City, Houston, and Ft. Worth are experimenting with this concept which fuses three ideas into one: (1) small groups, (2) pastoral care groups, and (3) task groups. Time will tell what shape this experiment will eventually take but already indications point toward a more vibrant congregation where house churches and small groups are utilized.

Basic to implementing many of the ministries in the church today is an understanding of small groups. This book is written to assist persons who want to learn more about small groups and their possibilities for bringing renewal and outreach to the local church.

DEFINITIONS

"A personal group is a small number of persons (four to twelve) meeting face-to-face regularly for the purpose of the study of the Bible [scriptures] and of the Christian faith; for prayer; for the exchange of experiences, needs, and insights; and for taking thought as to how they can best fulfill their calling as Christians to love and serve God and other people."–John Casteel

"The small group is a laboratory in Christian experience where serious saints and interested friends meet to explore scripture, pray, and share each other's burdens in a mutual search to know God's will and carry it out."–T. Ed Barlow

ACKNOWLEDGMENTS

I cannot begin to adequately express my gratitude to the many friends who have helped to mold the convictions expressed here. However, I must include a note of special thanks to Dr. Roy Cheville, presiding patriarch of the church, who read my first few pages of notes and encouraged me to write the book. His criticism and suggestions were especially helpful on several chapters.

Dr. Gerald Knutson, pastor at Stillwater, Oklahoma, and staff administrator at Oklahoma State University, a good friend and critic, gave helpful advice on the manuscript. Dr. Howard Clark, pastor at Ft. Worth and head of the psychology department at Texas Wesleyan University, made suggestions as we shared in workshops. Two Oklahoma City pastors—Stan Norcom and Dennis Clevenger—assisted by initiating small group activities in their congregations and sharing prayer breakfasts for several months.

I wish to thank the publishers listed on the following page for permission to quote copywrited material.

Three typists have given hours of labor. Carol Hawkins in Tulsa typed the original draft and many redrafts of the manuscript. Her husband, Howard, gave valuable assistance with the data in the statistical section of Chapter 12 before it was fed into the computer. My co-worker in the missionary office in Oklahoma City, Elder B. A. Howard, helped with typing and checked references. The final copy was typed by Shirley Clevenger, one of several dedicated volunteers in the Oklahoma City District Missionary Office. To all these I say "thanks."

Special gratitude is due Jim and "Snooky" Holt who allowed me to use their cabin on Lake Tenkiller in eastern Oklahoma for several days while completing the manuscript.

And most of all to my wife Marjorie and our four children, who so often have had to manage at home without me in order that others might receive ministry, I express profound appreciation.

The following publishers have granted permission to quote copyrighted material:

Guideposts Associated, Inc., Carmel, New York 10512
    (1) "How High Is Your Spiritual Outreach?" February 1962, *Guideposts Magazine*
    (2) "What to Do When" from booklet *The Small Group a Big Answer,* page 16

Faith at Work
1000 Century Plaza, Suite 210
Columbia, Maryland 21043
    Quotes from *Faith at Work Handbook* and *Open Circle*

Downe Publishing, Inc.
641 Lexington Avenue
New York, New York 10022
    "Listening" by Brenda Ueland, *Ladies Home Journal,* November, 1941

Word Books Publisher
4800 West Waco Drive
Waco, Texas 76703
    Quotations from *Witnessing Laymen Make Living Churches,* by Monro & Taegel

INTRODUCTION

The church today is being pressed to discover its mission and find creative ways to expand its fellowship. Many are searching for modern structures which congregations can utilize to achieve these two objectives. The small group meeting is increasingly coming to the front as one answer.

Elton Trueblood believes the small group approach is one of two keys to the single most significant religious movement in this century. Speaking to a conference of ministers early in 1971 at Oklahoma City, he said he felt this would go down in history as the century of "church renewal." At first, some believed the ecumenical movement would be the chief characteristic of the twentieth century. Now there are clear indications that the recent stirrings within the established churches aimed at spiritual "renewal" will be remembered as the outstanding religious event of the 1900's.

When I heard this respected religious leader say that one key to this renewal was *lay ministry* I felt a warm confirmation of the ministerial concept which the Restoration Church has always emphasized. The Saints have functioned from the beginning with a self-supporting priesthood. Dr. Trueblood then said the second key to renewal was the phenomena of "small groups." Fortunately there are indications that within the next decade many persons in the Saints Church will see the tremendous value of the small group meeting.

During the last ten years I have increasingly felt that this method holds great possibilities for the church. It is more a "sharing" than a "telling" method which can make congregational life more relevant to the needs of people.

I have been involved in over a thousand small group meetings, and I have seen many persons deeply affected by the gospel as they were introduced to it in these fellowships.

I agree with Bruce Larson and Ralph Osborne who, in *The Emerging Church,* say:

"The life of the congregation in the emerging church will probably be structured around *small groups* of believers. That is, the interrelationships of people in dialogue is the means by which Christ may most clearly make himself and his purposes known."

Sam Shoemaker lists six sources of power available to people trying to live the Christian life. After mentioning prayer, corporate worship, the Bible, and Holy Communion, he lists the fifth source of power as *fellowship.* Of it he says:

"Then comes the deeper kind of fellowship which many want, all need, and few find. Frankly, where I see young Christians growing and going ahead most today are the places where *small groups* gather regularly with the best leadership afforded to study, pray, and exchange ideas until each of them becomes effective in making faith real to other people. . . . *Women* should be brought together in small groups for prayer which so deepens their spiritual life that they become transmitters of the faith to others by life and by word. *Men* should be brought together in small groups for exchange of experience which steadily transforms their life. Let half a dozen men and women come together for prayer and making spiritual friends with one another, meet steadily, study, work, until they become a team, and you will find a power in the company which is very much more than the sum of the power you will find in the individual: 'two or three' is the condition for his Presence. The Holy Spirit seeks 'the company' to work in and through. Not all will be ready for this deeper kind of experience, but some will, and the church must change its gears and learn to provide for this great need of fellowship at a deeper level for its people."— Shoemaker, *How to Become a Christian,* Harper and Row.

In 1971 when the Oklahoma City Metropolitan District leaders went into retreat to establish goals for the next five years, they listed Objective No. 3 as "creating contemporary forms for witnessing, redemptive, and teaching ministries in congregational life." Small groups were clearly among these contemporary forms. In the Oklahoma City District there are now a number of small groups meeting weekly to pray, read scripture, share personal struggles, and grow in the faith. One form of these groups is called "house churches." These groups focus on home ministry, mission, and fellowship functions of the church. Some small groups meet in prayer circles, some for prayer breakfasts, and others as discussion groups. They take many different forms. Whatever the structure, wherever such meetings are held the church seems to come alive as the Saints pray and share the good news with one another.

CHAPTER ONE

OUTREACH AND RENEWAL THROUGH SMALL GROUPS

The more one studies the New Testament church and identifies key characteristics of that fellowship, the more one is impressed with the need for modern structures to facilitate the kind of life the early disciples experienced. The quality of their association and the presence of the Holy Spirit know no time or cultural barriers. Their experience of love and union with one another is universal, and it is available now if the modern church can catch the same spirit of commitment and provide the structures which will facilitate this style of life.

Small groups are seen increasingly as a vital factor in the renewal of the church. If the modern church is to maintain vitality or deepen its spiritual life, many small companies of committed people will be required who are honest with God and open to each other in a fellowship characteristic of the New Testament church.

Someone reported that Billy Graham was once asked how he would proceed if he were asked to win a large city for Christ. He responded by saying he would select twelve men and meet regularly with them until they understood the vision and strategy for winning the city. These men with others would carry out the program (small groups) which Jesus first used.

Howard A. Snyder in an article in *Christianity Today* (November 6, 1970) puts it this way:

"The idea of the Koinonia of the Holy Spirit, then, suggests that the church should provide structures

1. In which believers gather together.
2. Where intercommunication is encouraged.
3. In an informal atmosphere that allows the freedom of the Spirit.
4. In which direct Bible [scripture] study is essential.

"Most contemporary church patterns and structures clearly do not meet this criteria, but there is one structure that does—some form of the *small group*. It is my conviction that the Koinonia of the Holy Spirit is most likely to be experienced where Christians meet together informally in such small group fellowships."

Because of their limited size and informality small groups provide an excellent setting for communication. George Weber in *Congregations and Missions* notes, "No relationship of love can develop unless there is structure in which it can grow." Bruce Larson, president of Faith at Work, says in *The Emerging Church:*

"When Christians experience the grace of God during the week by doing the will of God, *being in small groups,* trying to find ways to be obedient to their families and on their jobs, then we can lead them in a celebration on Sunday in what has been happening during the week. But what we frequently find is people who have not had an experience with Christ during the week coming to church to 'have an experience.' That's all wrong, and we shouldn't let that kind of expectation—that wanting to turn the Sunday services into a makeup period on the subject of God—dominate our Sunday services. We don't come to church on Sunday to experience God but to celebrate the fact that we have been with him through the week in various ways."

Small groups make this kind of experience possible.

Phillip Watson observes that originally the Methodist Church began as small groups within the Church of England:

"In order to make and keep a living reality, Wesley divided his societies up into classes. These were groups of not more than ten members who met together once a week under the leadership of one of their own number for conversation, discipline, prayer, and growth in the spiritual life.

"The class meetings were not study circles, not discussion groups, and least of all were they debating societies. They were Christ-centered fellowships. Their members were taught to take seriously the Lord's promise that he would be present in their midst 'wherever two or three were gathered together in his name.' Hence, when they met in class they would sing, they could go on to share their Christian experience with one another—their troubles, triumphs on the Christian way, or on their quest for that way. Sometimes they confessed their sins to one another, sometimes took one another to task, always with the aim of helping one another to grow in grace, in faith and hope and love. Their varying degrees of spiritual maturity enabled them all the more to help one another by mutual conversation and prayer and it was, of course, understood that no one would gossip about anything said in class."—*Message from the Wesleys*, pages 51-52.

Bruce Larson comments on another occasion:

"The rebirth of a biblical theology in most of the biblical denominations of today has resulted in a commitment-centered message. I genuinely rejoice in it, but it is not enough. One more altar call, decision card, church officer's retreat, or campfire surrender won't do it. Something else is needed. A fellowship must exist where committed people can begin to be honest with one another and discover the dimension of an apostolic fellowship."—*Honesty Is the Only Policy,* pamphlet by Faith at Work.

A small group meeting can be a laboratory in Christian experience where serious Saints and friends explore scripture, pray, and share one another's burdens. They stimulate positive change, growth, maturity, and wholeness. The need for these small group meetings in the life of the church is becoming more obvious. Past fears due to excesses in some areas where inexperienced or unskilled persons attempted group meetings must no longer delay the utilization of a method which is time-tested and proved by experienced spiritual giants of past centuries.

Jesus is our best authority on small groups. He chose twelve "to be with him." It was the training of this small group upon which he based his whole hope for the future kingdom. The early church prospered as the book of Acts reveals, with little groups meeting in homes here and there and living a life of shared possessions and mutual support. When the church was spiritually vibrant, the members were very close to each other.

A recent study in the Texas-Oklahoma Region by Stan Norcom comparing congregational size with annual baptismal increases showed not only that large congregations diminish in percentage of baptisms as they get beyond a certain numerical enrollment level but that the actual number of persons baptized decreased. I am not advocating that we have small congregations but rather that we provide structures within the large congregations whereby the intimate association enjoyed by the small congregations will not be lost as the numerical strength of the group continues upward.

The small group is effective because it is established on basic principles of human nature. Therefore, it can be applied to any culture or area of church life. The theory behind it is that the gospel is more "caught than taught." Religion is not a list of facts or propositions to get across to people as much as it is an experience and encounter with a loving Father in heaven. The best way to communicate this love and relationship is to bring a friend into a climate where persons are already in contact with God. The friend is more apt to catch the Spirit of the Christ in this exposure. The small group attempts to set up circumstances where this "catching" process can begin. Christian experience is more a focal concern than doctrine or theology. This is not to deny the value of theology and doctrine. The question is, "Do we give them doctrine first and hope they have an encounter later, or do we help to create the climate for encounter first and then give them doctrine afterwards to explain the meaning of the experience?" Doctrine is very important; it must always be in the picture—but often it follows rather than precedes "the encounter." Many converts say they were actually "loved" into the church.

Because man is made in the image of God, every person has a deep longing for Christ even though he may not recognize what the longing represents at any given moment. Truth tends to be attractive within itself to those who are repentant and seeking. People tend to respond if they can be properly exposed to the gospel in its simple beauty in an unthreatening atmosphere. The small group attempts to expose people (in and out of the church) to the goodness of Christ and the gospel with no pressure, pushing, or cajoling. Often Christ can best be revealed in warm personal relationships.

"One has to experience what is happening in a group

to realize how God can work where there is an aggregation of people with faith, with prayers going up and grace coming down, and the cross lines between people are multiplying and strengthening so [they] are finding both new friends and depth in the Lord. Dr. Achenheil of the University of Pittsburgh, reflecting the need of the nation for a personal change, says in a pithy sentence, 'The cell group is the way to get and dispense information on God and Country.' "–Samuel Shoemaker, *Beginning Your Ministry*, Harper & Row, 1963, page 73.

Modern men today tend to be alone, isolated from each other. The affluence, commercialism, industry, and rush of an impersonal generation is taking its toll in suicides, nervous breakdowns, and warped personalities. The human soul seeks to know others and be known. In a small group meeting concerned Christians can be moved from their felt need of depth communication on to the Source of all souls–God. The small group can be the bridge from isolation to the fellowship of the church.

A convert needs special support during the first months of enlistment in his new life in the church. If he has come in by way of a small group he already has loving, caring people around him who know his inner needs. The strength of several concerned persons is of great value to one just beginning a totally new way of life. Assimilation into the church is easier when one moves from the small group fellowship than when he tries to start out completely alone. People can learn the elementary lessons of caring in the warmth of a small group. After one's ability to love and care is opened up to new dimensions in a small group, it can be expanded to include the whole church.

Several years ago when I first became acquainted with Alcoholics Anonymous, I was impressed with a number of things. One amazing thing I noticed was the speed with which a person asking for help could get A.A. members to respond and come to his aid even though they had never met him before. I once had occasion to counsel a church member with an alcoholic problem. I talked him into calling A.A. On the other end of the phone was a concerned man (A.A. member) reaching out to assist. Within the hour my friend had four telephone calls from other concerned A.A. people, and before I left he had been invited to a meeting that night. My mind turned to the church, and I wondered if the day would ever come when we would be able to care for people in a spiritual way with the expertise of Alcoholics Anonymous.

One experience I can point to where this happened to some degree occurred a few years ago in Tulsa. A pastor's wife phoned long distance from a town some miles away because she was concerned about a nonmember niece in Tulsa who was in need of help. I called the pastor of Tulsa Central, George Hayworth, and the next night this niece was in a small group meeting—a mere twenty-four hours after the long distance call. Small groups can serve many purposes in a congregation. One is to provide a place for troubled people who are in urgent need of relating to concerned Christians who can help them to find identity and gain spiritual strength. If we had had to organize a group in Tulsa after receiving that long distance call this young woman would not have received the help and strength which the group was able to give her within twenty-four hours. Someday we will be organized and ready to receive people in need when many small groups are meeting on different nights of the week.

"It is true that small groups do not automatically bring vitality, nor do they necessarily encourage people to become lay apostles. A group can be sick, deadly, oppressive, sterile, or unreal. Nevertheless, we do not know of a single church now producing live laymen that does not have at its heart some form of small group program of fellowship.

"In small groups, whatever they are called or however they are constituted, there must be several components. At some point of the weekly or biweekly meeting there must be a time when people can open their hearts to one another to talk about their past failures and present hopes. It is through this ministry of confessing to one another (which is affirmed time and again in the scripture) that we find God bringing healing to his people.

"There must also be a place in the small group for dialogue and encounter wherein members can discern gifts among one another which might never be discerned otherwise. It is amazing how limited we are in seeing ourselves without the help of others. Anyone who begins to live with a few others, as unto Christ, begins to find out things about himself that he would never see alone, in private worship or meditation."—Larson and Osborne, *The Emerging Church,* pages 94-95.

The Garden Grove Community Church, Orange County, California, is a very large Protestant congregation. Harold Leestma, one of the ministers on the staff in charge of evangelism, reports in *The Emerging Church:*

"Our laymen leadership team has grown to seventy persons in charge of thirty-two small fellowship groups. They meet in living rooms, around kitchen tables, in coffee shops, and on the church campus. Every two months I meet with these leaders for an exciting time of sharing experiences, which gives me a chance to examine the pulse rate for each group. This leadership team is under the auspices of our evangelism committee that meets with me every month to plan overall guidance.

"The fear is sometimes expressed that home groups will become ingrown and separate themselves from the life of the church as a whole. This has not happened at Garden Grove. The home groups have helped our people to relate more naturally and comfortably to the total church program. In finding themselves, individuals are more free to lose themselves in others.

"As for service in the church, it has tripled. Even very shy people are stepping forward seeking their particular assignments from God. Believing that God has a definite plan for each life they often cannot wait to get into action.

"Jesus Christ is alive! With his power working in us, we come alive, too. Live people make live churches."

Here is a good example of a church that did not have to become small to become personal and relevant.

George Webber, in *God's Colony,* puts it this way:

"This new focus in the life of the colony goes under many different names: small group, study group, house meetings, and so on. I dislike most of these phrases, for too often their emphasis is a narrowly biased one or basically turned inward to the church and not outward to the task of preparing the Christian for his work in the world. Whatever we call the small group I'm talking about—the second focus of the life to the congregation—it must have as a strenuous emphasis, preparing its members for the concrete task which they face outside the life of the colony. It must not be designed to make us more pious or simply to instill more knowledge about our faith."

At one time Charles Wesley set forth the value of small groups as follows:

"Many other advantages have flowed from this closer union of believers with each other. They prayed one for another that they might be healed of the faults that they confessed, and it was so. The chain was broken; the bands were burst asunder, and sin had no more dominion over them! Many were delivered from the temptations out of which up to then they had found no way of escape. They were built up in our most holy faith. They rejoiced in the Lord more abundantly. They were strengthened and loved and more effectively provoked to abound in every good work."—W. Curry Madis, *Advancing the Smaller Church,* page 15.

George A. Buttrick believed that the hope of a genuine spiritual awakening in our day lies in the small religious group. He said, "Real revival has always begun in a little group that defied the values of the world and lived under a new and stringent discipline of life" (from an address before the Chicago Sunday Club reported in the *Christian Century,* February 29, 1956).

Elton Trueblood sees great contemporary significance in small religious groups. He believes they are the hope of the world, an alternative to the futility of the present age. Trueblood holds that Western civilization can be saved by "little redemptive societies" of spiritually concerned Christians. The best chance of the renewal of the human spirit in the twentieth century, as in the first, lies in the formation of genuinely redemptive societies in the midst of ordinary society. Trueblood says minimum requirements for membership in such societies are as follows:

"1. Commitment to Christ.
"2. Willingness to witness to another.

28

"3. Genuine fellowship.

"4. Willingness to perform Christian work.

"5. Personal discipline."

—*Advancing the Small Church*, pages 18, 19.

William T. Ham of the Church of the Savior, Washington, D. C., says:

"Only where a small group of disciples is gathered in his name is he present with that peculiar power which he promised his followers. That is to say the existence of a small group of persons committed to Christ and bound together in a special Christian fellowship is a necessary condition for the coming of the Holy Spirit. Large groups can ordinarily be so blessed only when there exists within them such dedicated groups of disciples."

In such a small group, by the aid of the Holy Spirit, one may recapture the vision and power of the little band that centered around Jesus. Except for its leader that group was a fellowship of ordinary, weak, fallible men. One was a traitor, one a coward; others were crudely ambitious. When the crises came they all fled. Yet, obscure as they were, within twenty years of the death of Jesus people in faraway Macedonia were saying that they were turning the world upside down. Within three hundred years, the Roman Empire bowed to their movement.

"That first group fellowship, like those that came after it, was animated by a spirit of love and of loyalty. [The members] devoted themselves to the instructions given by the apostles to fellowship and break bread and pray together (Acts 2:42). Out of that came their tremendous spiritual power. Their fellowship was not merely a fellowship among themselves nor was it a fellowship of the believers individually with God. Their attitude toward God was reflected in their attitude toward their Christian brethren. And their attitude toward their Christian brethren was patterned after God's attitude to them. They loved others as Christ loved them—not for the sake of being loved in turn, but in order to help others to win salvation. They loved redemptively."—John Casteel, *Spiritual Renewal Through Personal Groups,* pages 167-168.

Sometimes an individual will ask, "How many were baptized as a result of these small group meetings?" Baptisms are not the symbol of success of any method. Results in this category, however, are often positive. A brief check of a few small groups in Oklahoma revealed that these adults were in a series of small group discussions leading up to their decision to be baptized:

1. Ken and Doris________had their first church contact in a small group meeting. Both were baptized. He's now an elder and leads a small group (prayer breakfast) on Saturday mornings.
2. Marjorie ________'s husband was a member. She attended group meetings and was baptized.
3. Kate________was a Mormon. She had no previous ties to the church. Her first church contact was a discussion group.
4. Butch________'s wife was a member. He seldom attended church before the small group meetings were started. He was baptized and later ordained.
5. Reta ________'s husband was an inactive member. Both attended small group meetings. She decided to be baptized.
6. Mona ________'s in-laws were in the church. She was afraid of all churches but felt accepted in the warm

fellowship of the small group and became a positive contributor in the discussions. After meeting weekly with the group for six months she was baptized.

7. Brenda _______ was engaged to a church member. She attended a youth discussion during series and was baptized soon afterwards.

8. Susie _______ had no previous religious ties. College students witnessing introduced her to the church. She enjoyed the warm fellowship and joined in the discussions. Later she decided to join the church.

9. Judy _______ had no previous association with the church. She began attending and was asked to teach a church school class. She might have been baptized anyway but says she got help in a discussion group.

10. Leslie _______'s husband was a deacon. After attending several small group meetings she made her decision to be baptized.

11. Don _______'s wife was a member. He attended a discussion on Sunday evening and also had a cottage meeting in his home. He was baptized.

12. Willa _______'s husband was an inactive member. She attended a discussion group and later was baptized.

13. Connie _______ married an RLDS member. She felt the Spirit first in a small group, was baptized and then became involved in active work.

The following comments were made by people (three of them nonmembers at the time) who attended small group meetings held in Oklahoma.

Mona Colson went to meetings at the home of her sister-in-law for one year. (She is now a member.)

"The informality and fellowship of the meeting put me at ease even though I was a nonmember. Slowly I built up courage to ask questions and give some opinions of my own. I felt some of my questions on religion were stupid, but it had been said in the group that no questions concerning Jesus Christ or the Bible were considered stupid. I think we have all learned many things from these discussions. . . . I know I have. Also we learned to know and appreciate each other. I am still learning and am thankful for this opportunity."

Edna McManus had had no ties to the church until her teen-age daughter joined.

"I have been attending the Bible-study group now for about five months, and I have learned much. I have felt more wanted by this group than anywhere else. I look forward to the meeting, appreciate it more each week, and would like for it to continue. I am grateful for the feeling of being welcome in the homes of the group members. I feel I need this experience very much to learn more about God. It helps me understand my children and be a better mother and person. I want to keep learning."

Kate Poulter was baptized after attending discussion group sessions for a while.

"I felt very close to the people in our group. They had such a love for each other; anyone could feel free to ask questions and get help to problems. The group helped me learn about the church and make my decision to join. I am very happy; for the first time in years I am able to feel the Spirit. The circle prayers at the close of meetings are very meaningful to me."

Mike Hamel said:

"This small group in the Del City, Oklahoma, branch has shown me that I don't have to hold priesthood to be concerned for, to love, and to minister to my fellow Saints. I have learned that the Lord *really can* use my talents! The small group has helped me grow spiritually."

Connie Hamel was won to the church through the small group.

"I was just baptized three months ago at Del City, Oklahoma. The small group meeting I attended with my RLDS husband was more meaningful to me than the formal meetings at church. I felt the Spirit more in our small groups than anywhere I had ever been. Now that I am a member I enjoy both the small groups and the formal church worship services. The small group was the beginning of my interest in the restored church."

The testimony of Elder Bruce A. King cites the value of group discipline.

"The small discipline group is my chief source of spiritual strength. It is the high point of my week. Through the love and concern of others in the group I have been able to discipline my life to pray with direction, fast with a purpose, study with insight, and praise the Lord for everything in my life. Without this group I would die spiritually."

In every age the church utilizes methods appropriate to the day to communicate the gospel. The principles of the gospel of Christ are eternal and never change. The "package" in which this gospel is communicated must continually evolve to meet the needs of each generation. The small group is suited for this generation. It is already being used by many organizations. Its worth has been proved. While still relatively new to some churches it is being increasingly utilized as a basic tool to expand the fellowship.

The attempts at personal witnessing, visitation, in-church meetings, and mass evangelism all have had their place. The potential for evangelism through the small group, however, has yet to be fully realized.

Renewal and spiritual vitality are being experienced in many churches today. University students who meet regularly for Wednesday morning breakfast in Norman, Oklahoma, are giving life to a mission. In their weekly sessions they go over a chapter in one of the Gospels, pray together, share their needs, problems, and hopes, then commit themselves deeply to each other and Christ.

At Stillwater, Oklahoma, students from the State University meet early one day each week for "un-breakfast" (fasting). Lives are being changed and vitality brought to the congregation because of them. All over the country new life is coming to the churches where the old idea of informal small group meetings is being introduced. Del City, Oklahoma, has a small group of young adults meeting emphasizing spiritual disciplines. Converts are being won and members renewed.

The "Witnessing Weekend," now being held in many churches by a visiting team, needs follow-up and stability for the congregation to experience lasting benefit. The formation of small groups following a weekend is an excellent way to provide for continued growth. Preceding a preaching mission or campaign small groups discussing the sermon topics in informal home meetings can provide the personal touch to large mass meetings. Follow-up after the mass meetings is best accomplished in small groups.

CHAPTER TWO

INCREASE OF INTEREST IN SMALL GROUPS

Interest in small groups has exploded on many fronts in the past two decades. Invading practically every segment of society, the small group method is being employed by industry, psychology, education, religion, and even in such areas as teaching students to play the piano.

The rapid rise of interest in small groups seems to parallel the rapid development of industrialization. Along with that development has come an increased depersonalization of society. As the population has shifted to large urban centers, and technology has advanced at breathtaking speed, there has been a corresponding dehumanizing effect on people. Intimate interaction between persons at significant levels has been replaced by superficial contacts in factories and on crowded streets. This has caused an "interpersonal vacuum" to exist for many. People have been driven toward situations and circumstances where meaningful relationships could be established.

The rapid rise of therapy-type group meetings in the last few years is an indication of the loneliness of millions. The popularity of sensitivity, encounter, and T-groups indicates that people are crying out for identification, relatedness, and meaningful contact.

Some excesses and abuses will attend any quickly conceived idea, especially when it is reached for in desperation. Such has been the case in the small group field. Untrained leaders, under the guise of professionalism, have brought unfortunate results. Some have gone off on tangents. Some have made overzealous claims. Every new idea (or in this case old idea rediscovered) carries with it the threat of abuse by unskilled and unwise persons. Some who have attended meetings have been turned off because of the misuse of the small group technique. The church cannot afford to be turned away from it because of these unfortunate experiences.

Small group meetings employ principles consistent with the nature of human personality and therefore work in all cultures. This is of tremendous significance to the church as it moves into different nations.

It has been estimated that the Methodist Church has over five thousand small group meetings being held in homes in the United States every week. Early in 1971 Oklahoma Methodists held a statewide conference at which Dr. Elton Trueblood was the guest speaker. The entire conference was devoted to helping Methodist clergy and laymen discover the powerful ministry possible in small groups. I was privileged to share in this conference and saw many members and ministers eagerly exploring this means of renewal.

The Catholic Church has published two books, *Living Room Dialogues,* to be used in a program of informal discussions to which nonmember neighbors are invited for a discussion of ideas, common beliefs, and practices. The Presbyterians devoted the July issue (1969) of their publication, *Christ in Missions,* to the small group movement. *Faith at Work* magazine for more than three decades has been supplying information about small groups and how they can be used to deepen faith and spread the gospel. Other lay-oriented movements such as Faith at Work (Columbia, Maryland) and the Institute of Church Renewal (Atlanta, Georgia) aim at equipping the church member to lead small groups and extend the effectiveness of the church. Practically every denomination in America is utilizing the small group in some form to further its goals and objectives.

Missionaries returning from the Orient report that the "Rinsho Kosei Kai," a Buddhist lay movement in Japan, is spreading faster than any other religion. It is based primarily on the small group approach. The "Hora" is a separate group meeting in a home to discuss Buddhist teachings as they apply to everyday situations; these informal home meetings are very popular. People meet and talk about personal needs and problems, discovering from each other how to relate these to their faith. The groups grow and divide. This religion is rapidly gaining followers while the more highly structured institutions are struggling to keep their members.

Many people are unaware of the rise of interpersonal groups and their significance. Yet increasing numbers of observers say with Paul Hare, "Everywhere I turn the small group is being rediscovered."

John Casteel says:

"Small interpersonal groups are becoming the basic units for carrying on the functions of our society. In corporation structures, advertisements, scientists, technicians, and engineers all emphasize the team concept. A new process for increasing potential creativity in solving theoretical and technical problems, called 'synectics,' depends on the small group as a basic working unit."

In the foreword to the book *Groups Alive—Church Alive,* Casteel says:

"The intensive group experience has been said to be, perhaps, the most significant social invention of this century. Certainly Carl Rogers is right in calling it one of the most rapidly growing social phenomena in our nation. Small groups have 'exploded' into every part of our social order—institutional and organizational, corporate, educational, and religious."

John Drakeford analyzed some common features found in many self-help groups such as Alcoholics Anonymous; Tops; Recovery, Inc.; and Synanon. He discovered, among other things, the principle of honest sharing utilized by good small group leaders—a feature common to most successful methods of changing behavior. Alcoholics Anonymous has probably been the most successful movement in this century to help people overcome severe personality problems. Small informal class group meetings are utilized by A.A. to facilitate honesty and openness in their effective spiritual approach to helping people in deep need of change.

Bruce Larson and Ralph Osborne describe it this way:

"We live in a time when small groups are being rediscovered as a primary means of enabling both clergy and laity for mission. A small group is a place where personal healing can come to individuals through sharing of experience, Bible study, and prayer."—*The Emerging Church,* page 146.

The alert person can sense that the shift in society today is toward the small informal group. The church of the future will be increasingly pushed to learn effective ways to employ small groups in congregational life.

A growing number of church jurisdictions are introducing the small group method of ministry into their training programs. Various names are given to the method in different denominations, but regardless of the name all refer to one of the fastest growing procedures in Christian education today.

CHAPTER THREE

SMALL GROUPS IN EARLY YEARS

Long before the church owned buildings or used visual aids in proselyting a small group of friends meeting in a home to hear firsthand testimony was effective in propagating the faith. Anyone reading church history becomes aware of the many small gatherings of relatives and friends at which the gospel was discussed. Today churches are moving to recast this old method in a contemporary mold.

Jesus had the twelve and an inner group of three. He worked closely with this circle of men to deepen their understandings about the kingdom and strengthen their commitment to one another. The principle is very old and fundamentally sound.

"The genius of the Methodist movement, which enabled it to conquer the raw lives of workingmen in industrial England, and the raw lives of men and women on the American frontier, was the 'class meeting'—ten members and their leader, meeting regularly for mutual encouragement, rebuke, nurture, and prayer."—John Casteel, *Spiritual Renewal Through Personal Groups,* American Book-Stratford Press, Inc., New York, 1957, page 20.

There is much support for the conclusion of Halford Luccock that "all the great movements in Christianity have been based on the training of small groups" (*Interpreter's Bible,* New York: Abingdon Cokesbury Press, 1951, Vol. 7, page 786). Jesus gave the promise for those in the setting of a small group: "Where two or three are gathered together in my name, there am I in the midst of them" (Matthew 18:20).

Recently a minister in Oklahoma said, "We are starting a new small discussion group in our congregation—but this isn't anything new. . . . We did it in our little mission on Sunday afternoon years ago." He had moved to the city from a small town in northeast Oklahoma. The intimate associations he had experienced in that little church had been lost since he had moved into the city and had begun attending a larger congregation. The small group was an attempt to recapture the situation and depth of fellowship which had brought him into the church.

John Casteel comments on the small group approach in the early history of the Christian Church:

> "In the revival of small face-to-face personal groups, the church really is returning to the kind of intimate associations which marked the earliest years of its history. To be a Christian, in the New Testament, is to belong to a company of people who share their life fully and deeply. The first description we have of the Church in the New Testament says, 'They devoted themselves to the apostles' teachings and fellowship and to the breaking of bread and to prayers' (Acts 2:42). To be a Christian at Ephesus or Colossae or Rome put you under temptations and demands peculiar to local conditions. But to belong to the church seemed to have brought you into common life wherever you might be. In Ephesus you are one of the church that met in the house of Aquila and Priscilla; in Colossae in the house of Nympha; in Rome, as one of 'Caesar's household.' You belong to an intimate band of men and women, who know that they have been lifted right out of their old life and into a new life. You meet together to listen to the scriptures, or the letters written by their leaders; to

pray; and to eat together at the table of their Lord. You are bound to one another by a common loyalty to Jesus Christ, and a common responsibility to and for one another that might require you to 'risk your neck' for one another. Nothing less than Paul's metaphor could describe what it means to be a Christian in the church; 'Now ye are the body of Christ and individually members in particular' (I Corinthians 12:27)."—*Spiritual Renewal Through Personal Groups.*

Keith Miller once scanned church history to examine the renewal movements and try to determine the key to them. He said he attempted to peel back the layers from the outward appearances of the reports and examine the renewal movement from within. He discovered in every great movement an almost identical pattern:

"One person in a local situation, who was usually not very important at the time, decided to give himself wholly to God with no strings attached. Then a few others gathered around this person, because a total conscious commitment by a sensitive individual eventually draws others into fellowship. It evidently makes people 'hungry' or 'homesick' for God."—*A Second Touch.*

Miller further observed that as these few people became deeply committed to the living Christ, a common vision came through. Gradually they found a particular shape their obedience would take in the world. He cites as examples Paul, Patrick of Ireland, Augustine, Francis of Assisi, Luther, Ignatius of Loyola, John Wesley, and George Fox. The most outstanding and least known (in Protestant circles) was Ignatius of Loyola (1491-1556). Loyola was a professional soldier in Spain who, when he was in his twenties, was injured in battle. In the hospital he came across devotional literature and was converted. His conversion so changed his life that he began to speak to others in the dormitory where he lived. He drew to himself a small group, perhaps a half dozen young laymen. One of his followers, Francis Xavier, later became one of the greatest missionaries in the entire church (Keith Miller, *A Second Touch*).

All of these examples point out how renewal comes through one or two persons who become deeply committed, then draw a small group around them to receive strength through their disciplined way of life and move out as led by the Spirit.

Small groups are as old as mankind. The family is the primary small group in society. Various forms have been utilized in every age. The present trend toward small groupings in all phases of contemporary society is only a modern accommodation of a very old idea. The sensitive churchman will recognize the universal appeal of the small group of committed persons meeting regularly for mutual strength, growth, and spiritual direction. The local congregation can experience renewal when serious disciples form small groups and meet regularly under the guidance of wise leadership.

CHAPTER FOUR

TYPES OF SMALL GROUPS

There are many types of small group meetings. Similar in basic ways, groups vary according to different objectives, leadership, needs and interests of the participants, and prevailing circumstances. The following are some types of small group meetings:

Study Discussion Groups. This is probably the most common and oldest type. It focuses on a text, topic, or some informational content. The American Institute of Discussion (International Headquarters in Oklahoma City) employs this technique in its study groups around the world. Some denominations have moved their church school programs almost entirely to the small group study-discussion type of meeting. The Catholic books mentioned earlier, *Living Room Dialogues,* were prepared for study discussion. Many groups discuss a chapter of scripture or some religious classic each meeting.

This type of group will have a moderator who facilitates participation by all members. Consideration is given to material which they have read before the meeting. Emphasis is on content, information, and ideas. There may be incidental sharing of personal experiences or feelings, but the primary goal is to stimulate conceptual understanding.

Robert Leslie (*Sharing Groups in the Church*) quotes Reuel Howe as warning about the futility of a fellowship of sharing which is devoid of any responsible study. Leslie suggests the following, however, as one method for study groups which also includes personal sharing related to the scriptures.

1. Read the scripture reference aloud using different voices for different characters where applicable and using modern translations freely (example, Genesis 37:2-8, 12:28, King James).

2. Discuss the associations stirred up in your mind by the passage of scripture. You are an expert on what associations come to your mind. Share these in as personal a way as you can with the study group. (If there are more than twelve in the group, divide into leaderless groups of about six.)

3. In groups of six, discuss the following question: "What do you think this story is really about in terms of a timeless, interpersonal incident?"

4. In the same groups of six, discuss your reaction to Genesis 45:5 ("God sent me before you to preserve life").

5. Discuss together in the larger group with the leader what it means to live a life directed by God. Other Bible stories and life situations can be handled similarly (example, Luke 19:1-9, story of Zaccheus). Leslie's suggestions make it possible to study and also include sharing.

Prayer Groups. Prayer groups are generally small in number. They meet often in homes but sometimes in the church--always for the purpose of praying together. Conversational prayer is frequently used. Rosalind Rinker has written several books introducing this easy, natural manner of prayer. Some groups aim primarily toward intercessory prayer; others focus on meditation; still others pray for personal needs. It is tragic that Restorationists, believing so strongly in modern revelation and the movement having been born in an experience of prayer, should have so few prayer groups. A personal tragedy or crisis sometimes motivates people to start one. These times of praying together are precious moments of communion. W. E. Sangster's little book, *Teach Me to Pray,* has helpful ideas on prayer groups.

44

Sharing Groups. A number of small groups meet for the purpose of sharing personal concerns and gaining strength to live the Christian life. The participants sometimes confess failures, mistakes, and fears, as well as hopes. The emphasis is on reporting to the group how Christ has moved in their lives since the last meeting. Self-examination and introspection are encouraged for the purpose of identifying barriers to spiritual growth. Through group prayer and sharing, these barriers can be removed, releasing persons for positive change and growth.

Occasionally an unskilled or unwise person will misuse such opportunity and thus color some minds against the whole small group process. All methods can be abused (including preaching, cottage meetings, and church school classes). In spite of such occasional excesses there remains great potential for ministry in the sharing groups. They can provide the setting for a positive sharing of hopes and dreams for the future. Ugly sins are not confessed, and participants are urged to leave out details. One soon learns in the sharing groups that he does not have to uncover all the bad in his life in order to share personally with others. Dr. Charles Mader of the University of Illinois (RLDS minister) explains how sharing requires understanding of others' goals. Sharing groups aim at the objective of deepening fellowship and facilitating personal awareness and growth in Christian faith.

Mission Action Groups. Many small groups are assembled primarily to accomplish a common task. These mission or task groups (sometimes called Zionic Action Groups) place primary emphasis on doing rather than talking. A single goal brings the group together; this may take the form of ministry to people with special needs (alcoholics, drug addicts, the elderly, shut-ins, unwed mothers). The dynamic interaction of the participants sharing in such service can deepen Christian unity. Sometimes such mission groups are of short duration, terminating when the goal is reached. Other groups are continued for varying lengths of time because the problem being attacked is a continuing one. The Church of the Savior in Washington, D.C., established by former Chaplain Gordon Cosby, is small and has a unique congregational structure. It is divided into mission groups, and everything which happens in the life of the church occurs in these groups with the exception of religious education and the worship service on Sunday. A mission group is started whenever some person feels the Holy Spirit guiding him to move in a particular direction of ministry (filling a human need). He has to clear this project with the church. Others are invited to pray and see if they feel the same "pull." If it is approved by the church, it is then supported by the rest of the membership. Every member of the Church of the Savior is involved in some type of mission group in which he expresses his basic Christian commitment. Even the pastor belongs to such a group.

Prayer Breakfast. Many businessmen on the way to work are meeting for prayer breakfasts. Usually these include a balance of scripture, personal sharing of needs for the day, and prayer for strength to cope with the secular environment. At Oklahoma City every Friday morning at 6:30 in Denny's Restaurant six men get together for depth sharing and prayer. They have been meeting for over two years. Similar prayer breakfasts are held in Mobile, Alabama, and Columbus, Ohio. (The university group in Norman, Oklahoma, has been mentioned already.) In an increasing number of places around the church Saints are seeking insight and strength for implementing Zionic ideals in the world of business—through this type of small group meeting.

Witnessing Groups. Some small groups are organized and meet primarily for the purpose of discussing and implementing a ministry of witnessing to friends outside the fellowship.

46

These groups study ways of reaching the unenlisted and cooperate with the pastor in programs of outreach. The Methodist Publishing House in Nashville, Tennessee, has special materials for witnessing groups. Claxton Monroe describes home witnessing groups in his Episcopal Church in Houston (*Witnessing Laymen Make Living Churches*, Word Books). Specific helps for Saints will soon be available.

Spiritual Growth Groups. These groups emphasize specific disciplines to deepen the spiritual life of the individual participants. They may study scripture or some of the religious classics for a broadened Christian perspective. Generally they agree to arise an hour earlier in the morning and spend a certain period of time in meditation, serve in specific ministry to other people, witness as guided by the Holy Spirit, and seek to follow guidance in daily decisions, then report to the group on the results. Elder Bruce King leads such a group in Del City, Oklahoma. This dynamic group has four basic disciplines: (1) daily prayer for each other, (2) fasting two meals each week, (3) study, and (4) praising God twice daily for everything, including trials and difficulties.

John Wesley describes his distinctive plan of small group organization which fits the spiritual growth definition:

"In compliance with their desire, I divided them into smaller companies; putting the married and single men, and married or single women together. The chief rules of these bands run thus: In order to confess our faults to one another, and pray for one another that we may be healed, we intend to

1. Meet once a week at least.
2. Come punctually at the hour appointed.
3. Begin with singing and prayer.

4. Speak each of us in order, freely and plainly, the true state of our soul, with the faults we have committed in thought, word, deed and the temptations since our last meeting.

5. Desire some person among us (thence called a leader) to speak his own state first, and the rest in order, and many searching questions as may be, concerning their state, sin, and temptations."— *Evolution of Protestantism.*

There are other types and variations of small group meetings. Types of meetings are limited only by the creative genius of the group leader. While each type differs slightly in format and purpose, all contain similar characteristics which place them in the same "small group" family. Basic principles of interaction and group support operate in all groups, regardless of name or purpose.

Congregational leaders can establish their own goals and utilize the types of groups which best meet their needs.

CHAPTER FIVE

CHARACTERISTICS AND ADVANTAGES OF SMALL GROUP MEETINGS

When I first became interested in small groups I was puzzled about the great variety of meetings yet realized there were some universal principles operating in all of them. Observation and reading on the subject revealed these common characteristics.

1. *The small group starts spontaneously.* It is generally not organized as other meetings are. A small group will arise out of some felt need for some particular persons. Leaders are usually prayerfully led to set up a meeting. It will not be successful if some ambitious administrator gets the idea the congregation ought to have more meetings and tries to organize groups as he would organize a class.

2. *The size of the meeting is limited.* The best number of participants seems to range from four to twelve people. Smallness is important because of the involvement objective. One goal is to have all members participate. A large group cannot achieve this.

3. *There are three basic ingredients in most groups.* These consist of (1) studying scripture, (2) sharing personal experiences, and (3) praying. Balancing these three is essential if the meeting is to be kept "alive" and healthy.

4. *There is an attitude of acceptance toward all in the group.* Everyone is encouraged to "be himself." Groups seek to remove the natural fear of criticism and

rejection. To achieve this atmosphere participants must be noncritical. Each person is permitted to have his opinion; however, no one else has to agree. An "open" atmosphere which helps facilitate free discussion is a common characteristic.

5. *Flexibility is essential.* Each meeting is different and must therefore be adaptable to varying situations. The needs of the members of the particular group are kept in mind as plans develop. Meetings may be weekly or bimonthly. Some are held at night, others in the daytime. Some are composed of one age group; others are mixed. Members do not all have to be of the same age, vocation, or interests to make a good group. The key factor is their common commitment to group objectives. It may even be helpful to have differences represented in the group if they are not too radical. Congenial persons do make leadership of the group easier.

6. *Listening is important.* People enjoy small groups where they can talk and be heard. One psychologist says you can measure how well you love people by how well you listen to them. Keith Miller explains that when you listen intently to another human being and really "hear him out" you are putting your hand quietly in his life and feeling gently along the rim of his soul until you come to a crack, some frustration, some problem or anguish you sense that he may or may not be totally conscious of. As you listen, you are loving this person and accepting him as he is. This factor in groups has great healing possibilities.

7. *Focus on scriptures is emphasized.* Scripture study is common to most all groups. Sometimes this may not be from an intellectual or informational point of view.

50

Usually small groups seek a depth understanding of what God is saying today through the scriptures. Often they stress experiential study rather than conceptual facts.

8. *Personal experiences are shared.* All group participants are encouraged to speak out openly, sharing their feelings as honestly as possible. This is a vital part of small group meetings, and its lack perhaps the cause of most group failures. Many persons seem willing to discuss scripture from an intellectual standpoint, but they are reluctant to relate it to themselves. The small group meetings which seem most "alive" are those in which people are free enough to share their inner world, including their fears, faults, doubts, and failures as well as their ambitions. When some member has had a real experience in prayer or has felt the Spirit of God moving in his life, the small group provides a climate for this to be shared.

> "I am obliged to bear witness, because I hold, as it were, a particle of light, and to keep it to myself would be equivalent to extinguishing it."—Gabriel Marcel

9. *Group members pray together.* Some may stand in a circle for the opening or the closing of a meeting, and some may kneel together. The question may be asked at the close of a meeting, "Do you know of anyone we ought to remember tonight? Do any of you have any special needs you want us to pray for?" Silent prayer, conversational prayer, or one or two volunteer prayers may be called for. Many groups like to say the Lord's Prayer in unison at the close of the meeting. Conversational prayer—the spontaneous yet directed thought-prayer—appeals to many people.

10. *Disciplines are agreed upon by common consent.* The agreed disciplines may be few but groups which have depth need them. As the group grows in spiritual maturity it will usually want to increase them. (See chapter on Disciplines.) Disciplines may include the following:

1. Attendance at church services
2. Daily devotions of prayer and scripture reading
3. Honest effort to commit oneself to Christ each day
4. Planned giving of tithes and offerings (and filing tithing statements)
5. A real effort to witness and win some specific persons to Christ and the kingdom
6. A sincere attempt to apply the Christ way in daily relationships (love, humility, truth, and faith in God)

The small group needs a balance. Sam Shoemaker has said that groups receive their depth from devotion and prayer and their dimension from witness and work.

Advantages of the Small Group

1. *Meetings are often attractive and "unthreatening" to the unchurched.* Members and nonmembers alike need to belong to some intimate group in which they can communicate deeply. It is much easier to get people to a small group discussion than a lecture or formal meeting at church. Great outreach opportunities are latent in good small group meetings.

2. *It offers personal ministry to everyone present.* The group can fill a definite need in each participant's life. The atheist, agnostic, nonmember, inactive member, active member, and priesthood can receive strength and help at the same time. The small group is not

aimed toward any particular category. All human beings need a closer walk with God.

3. *It can strengthen family life.* The small group can provide a ministry husband and wife can share. Children can participate. Communication within families can be deepened. Much activity in the church today separates families. This approach puts them together in a significant manner.

4. *It opens possibilities for more members to witness and be involved in specific evangelism.* Many who hold priesthood are not "slide men" or "chart men" and thus do little witnessing. This method requires only the scriptures. No mechanical equipment is needed; no lecture has to be memorized.

5. *It helps to integrate the convert into congregational life more quickly.* A recent convert needs support in his new life, especially during the first few months. People won in the small group already have a circle of friends who keep in touch for continued support and strength. The small group formed to bring about a conversion ought to continue for several weeks after the baptism for support and increased understanding for the new member.

6. *It teaches members how to witness.* People can learn how to talk (without talking too much) in small groups. Everyone has a story (of his encounter with God). Small groups open up tremendous new opportunities for members to witness to each other and to friends. The member can increase his skills in witnessing as he hears others' testimonies and gets feedback from his own.

7. *It helps persons realize the cost of discipleship.* The disciplines of church attendance, planned giving, daily

devotions, witnessing, etc., are a normal part of the small group. The new member has this awareness in the beginning of his spiritual journey. At baptism he already is practicing the disciplines essential for growth.

8. *Participants learn to pray publicly.* Frequently persons will offer their first public prayer in a small group. The group discipline of daily prayer encourages this vital Christian discipline among group participants.

9. *It prepares individuals for more effective worship experiences in church.* The background of the group experience prepares one for a more meaningful involvement in the corporate worship service.

10. *It provides the "Koinonia" of the church fellowship at a depth seldom found elsewhere.* Accepting the responsibility for others' lives and growth is one major purpose of the church. Power for such positive concern is released in small groups.

11. *It orients persons to riches within the scriptures.* Many people begin their serious reading of scriptures in small groups. Listening to others' interpretations broadens perspectives and expands understanding. An appreciation for the truths in the scriptures can be stimulated in the small group.

12. *It exposes people to the Holy Spirit found among committed disciples meeting in deep fellowship.* A greater awareness and sensitivity to the Spirit often result from small group meetings. Such experience can help a person understand the gospel as he "feels" God's love and catches the meaning of discipleship.

CHAPTER SIX

INTERPERSONAL RELATIONSHIPS

Few human beings can exist happily alone. People are made for fellowship and interaction. They grow and develop "in relation" to others. In church this is called fellowship. William Temple says: "If by the term 'fellowship' we denote the deliberate association of free persons, then it is true to say that personality is the capacity for fellowship." He further explains the tremendous value of being in deep relationship with people: "Mind will only perfectly discover itself in other minds; therefore fellowship is the true norm of value—and love its perfect realization." Small groups deepen interpersonal relationships.

The quality of one's relationships with others defines his life rather accurately. Any method or experience which deepens or enhances responsible interpersonal relationships among people is an advance toward the kingdom. The kingdom of God has been described as the "kingdom of right relationships." Reconciliation and loving relationships are at the heart of the gospel.

Sam Shoemaker explains three levels of fellowship:

". . . fellowship exists in three rings. (1) The outer ring is knowledge of each other, common names, and occupations, looks and personalities, acquaintance and friendship. (2) The second ring is a deeper knowledge of how each one thinks, feels, reacts; what he faces and what he is interested in: A growing feeling of being at home with him, comfortable, at ease. (3) The third and innermost ring is the bond of a long-range, perhaps lifetime fellowship-friendship lifted up to God to be used and infused by him; joys and sorrows gone through together; a creative, spirit-filled love. It goes without saying that such fellowship cannot exist apart from prayer, and every company committed deeply together experiences something of it."—*Under New Management*, Zondervan, p. 93.

Small group participants are more likely to contribute to the positive atmosphere in the meetings when they understand some of the principles of interpersonal relationships. As sure as gravity is a law of nature certain basic laws operate in the interpersonal field. I believe this from my own experience. A series of failures in personal relationships heightened my interest toward understanding the principles involved.

The six principles listed here have been drawn from scripture, insights from counseling, personal ministry, and involvement in small group meetings. While many statements could be formulated on the subject, these six are basic and help focus on key factors operating in the area of interactions between people.

Jesus, of course, gave the ultimate statement on interpersonal relationships when he expressed the two great commandments: love God with all your heart, might, mind, and strength and your neighbor as yourself. If this love were a ray of sunlight and it beamed through a prism splitting into six components they would be the following:

1. Acceptance

The first principle of interpersonal relationships is to express love to others as unconditional acceptance. Every human craves the no-strings-attached acceptance by other people. To love someone means to communicate acceptance.

The good news of the gospel is God's announcement,

through Christ, that he loves us and accepts us as we are now. We do not have to earn this love, but we must be willing to accept it. To grow in our relationship with God we must repent (turn toward him) and "accept God's acceptance" (Tillich's definition of faith).

To communicate love to a friend, member of the family, neighbor, brother in the faith, or stranger is to accept that person as he (or she) is now. This is much easier to say than to practice.

One of the most successful groups in helping people change behavior today is Alcoholics Anonymous. Members of A.A. seem to be able to experience acceptance of others and communicate it—especially to their fellow sufferers. This acceptance provides the basis for the start of a new life. The church ought to be an "accepting fellowship." Some congregations do not rate very high in the ability to accept persons of differing viewpoints or styles of hair and dress, particularly if they have deviant behavior.

A friend in Oklahoma reported his experience in an A.A. meeting one night. A woman came in desperate for help. She had been drinking, her clothes were dirty, her body smelled, and she was cursing. Some alert and caring A.A. member moved toward her and said, "We're glad you came." Another A.A. member offered her a cup of coffee. After the meeting was over someone else invited her to come back, and still another assured her, "We think we can help you." My friend turned to me in a challenging voice and asked, "Can you tell me of any other organization in town which would have been as accepting?"

"The Christian group, if it is genuinely Christlike, offers to each unique person complete acceptance. Acceptance is personal concern, listening love aimed at fully understanding and appreciating another person in the totality of his being, his desires, his motives, his feelings, his ideas, his words, and his actions. It is based not upon the person's attractiveness but upon God's ability to love him as he is."—Paul Miller, *Group Dynamics in Evangelism.*

Small groups can help people grow in the ability to accept other people unconditionally and at the same time not condone their deviant behavior. The best small group meetings are those where all people—non-Christians, members of different denominations, and fellow churchmen—feel accepted as they are.

What does it mean to accept others unconditionally?

1. It means allowing them to be themselves, regardless of circumstances.
2. It means treating them as persons of worth within their own right.
3. It means seeing them as having been created in the image of God.
4. It means doing nothing which would violate their agency.
5. It means loving them as they are *now*—not just when they measure up to some standard.
6. It means they can express their negative emotions or show their "seamy" side and still be accepted completely.
7. It means they are treated as "persons," not as objects to be manipulated . . . not as statistics or the means to an end.
8. It means holding human nature—and these people in particular—in high regard.
9. It means believing that one of the greatest freedoms in life is the freedom to be one's true self.
10. It means believing that when people are provided with

58

love in an atmosphere of unconditional acceptance they will tend to move toward maturity and growth.

11. It means believing that no one is free to change some inner parts of his soul until he feels accepted the way he is.

12. It means disapproving deviate behavior but accepting each person as a human being of great worth.

Thought Questions

1. Are there some type persons that "bug" you?

2. Do you know why they bother you?

3. Do you believe this statement: "Unless you can accept yourself as a unique individual you will not be able to accept other persons as unique and allow them to be different"?

4. Is there a relationship between how you feel toward yourself and how you feel toward others?

5. How does Christ help you to accept yourself?

6. How can you grow in your ability to accept people completely?

7. Why is it necessary for a group leader to be an accepting person?

2. Listening

The second principle of interpersonal relationship is to express love to others by uncritical *listening*.

Paul Tournier says one can measure love for others by how well he *listens* to them. If he really cares about them, he pays attention when they are ready to share their feelings.

Generally people are poor listeners. They don't really hear the other person out. Carl Rogers tells of his counseling experiences with troubled people. "When I listen un-critically," he says, "I often notice a moistness in their eyes as if they are saying, 'For the first time, someone really cares about my feelings and is listening.' " In a speech in Dallas, Texas, in 1967, Rogers described his view of the person reaching out for help as a person in a dungeon daily tapping a message on the wall, "Does anyone know I'm in here?" He says when we are willing to listen uncritically to that person it is like tapping a message back through the wall, "I hear you; I know you are there, and I care."

Karl Menninger, one of America's outstanding psychiatrists, said the biggest part of psychoanalysis is uncritical listening. People get sick if they are not heard. If they can find no one else to listen they hire a professional and pay an expensive fee in order to be heard. Listening is one important way to express love.

John Drakeford has written a book, *The Awesome Power of the Listening Ear.* In it he points out the tremendous effect listening has on people and how it is used in so many different areas to help people. Taylor Caldwell in *The Listener* says that even though they never see the listener, many people come to the room, tell their story, and receive help by feeling they have been heard.

Douglas Steers says, "To listen to another soul into a condition of disclosure and discovery may be almost the greatest service a human being may perform for another" (*The Creative Role of Interpersonal Groups in the Church Today,* edited by John Casteel, page 187).

Listening means
1. Hearing every word that is spoken.
2. Trying to understand what the person is saying.
3. Listening to the meanings behind the words.
4. Looking at the person while he is talking.
5. Listening to the expressions of the face, hands, and all gestures.
6. Trying to feel what he is saying.

60

7. Acknowledging by a nod, grunt, or smile that he is being heard.

8. Giving undivided attention to the one speaking.

9. Hearing him out to the end without interruption.

10. Encouraging him to communicate all he feels.

Dr. Menninger quoted Brenda Ueland on listening as the best expression he had found:

"Listening is a magnetic and strange thing, a creative force. . . . The friends that listen to us are the ones we move toward, and we want to sit in their radius as though it did us good, like ultraviolet rays. . . . When we are listened to, it creates us, makes us unfold and expand. Ideas actually begin to grow within us and come to life.

"It makes people happy when they are listened to. . . . When we listen to people there is an alternating current, and this recharges us so that we never get tired of each other. We are constantly being re-created.

"Now there are brilliant people who cannot listen much. They have no ingoing wires on their apparatus. They are entertaining but exhausting too. I think it is because these lecturers, these brilliant performers, by not giving us a chance to talk, do not let us express our thoughts and expand: and it is this expressing and expanding that makes the little creative fountain inside us begin to spring and cast up new thoughts and unexpected laughter and wisdom.

"I discovered all this about three years ago, and truly it made a revolutionary change in my life. Before that, when I went to a party I would think anxiously; 'Now try hard. Be lively. I would have to drink a lot of coffee to keep this up. But now before going to a party, I just tell myself to listen with affection to anyone who talks to me, to be in their shoes when they talk; to try to know them without my mind pressing against theirs, or arguing, or changing the subject. No. My attitude is: 'Tell me more.' This person is showing me his soul. It is a little dry and meager and full of grinding talk just now, but presently he will begin to think, not just talk automatically. He will show his true self. Then he will be wonderfully alive."—*Ladies Home Journal,* November, 1941.

Paul Tournier says the problem of modern man is loneliness. People need to communicate. They desire to be known and to know others in a deeply significant way. Listening is one of the greatest needs today. Small groups can help.

Thought Questions

1. Why is listening so important in leading group discussions?
2. Why is it sometimes hard to listen?
3. Do you agree that your love for a person can be measured by how well you listen?
4. How would you go about improving your listening capacity?
5. Can you expect others to listen to you if you do not hear them out regarding their feelings?
6. Do you feel there would be less misunderstanding between people if they listened more and communicated better?
7. Do you think it is a good idea for people to restate the previous speaker's position in a meeting where there are differences and emotions are reaching a high pitch? (Before an opposite position can be given, the speaker for the other side must restate the previous position to

the other man's satisfaction before he can begin his talk.)

8. How well do you listen?
9. How can you tell if someone is really listening to you?
10. Do you think others can tell when you are not really listening?

3. Openness—Humility

To relate successfully to others one must be genuine, open, and sincere.

The most severe condemnation Jesus gave in the three years of his ministry was aimed at people who pretended one thing but were in fact another. Everyone is familiar with the label "hypocrite." The opposite is sincerity, genuineness, honesty, or—in scriptural terminology—humility.

One vital characteristic in relating effectively to others is openness. Little children have this trait. One can always tell where they stand even though it may be to the embarrassment of their parents. As people grow older they learn to conceal their real feelings in order to get what they want. This develops a certain sociability, but with it often comes mistrust of others. This mistrust may be due to one's own untruthfulness. The more dishonest a person is the less he can relate effectively. Fearing rejection, people hide their true feelings. Adam and Eve hid in the garden after they had sinned. Concealment and sin often go together.

Small groups help create a climate in which persons can enter into honest sharing with one another and thus grow in maturity and spiritual insight. In *Transparent Self* Sidney Jourard says that people cannot know themselves (or others) without dialogue and self-disclosure to someone they trust. While believing it essential for growth and mental health he continues to warn, "I venture to say that there is probably no experience more horrifying and terrifying than that of self-disclosure to 'significant others' whose probable reactions are assumed but not known." No wonder some people are against small groups and the concept of openness! There are risks, but Keith Miller says the alternative is death!

"To be able to receive a gift you have to know how to open yourself. But when a person is making the gift of himself, then it is very hard—for to receive him you have to give yourself. You cannot possess a person; you cannot count a person among your goods. To receive someone who is giving himself to you, you have to give yourself to him just as fully, just as earnestly as you want him."—Ezley, *Our Prayer,* Herder and Herder, page 11.

Paul Tillich says:

"When two persons try to communicate with one another with less than their whole being, they cannot really respect one another and cannot understand one another. . . .

"A self which has become a matter of calculation and management has ceased to be a self. It has become a thing."—*The Courage to Be,* Yale University Press, 1953.

God spoke these words to the ancient American prophet Moroni:

"If men come to me, I will show them their weakness. I give men weakness that they may be humble; and my grace is sufficient for all men that humble themselves before me; for if they humble themselves before me and have faith in me, then will I make weak things become strong to them."—Ether 5:27-28.

To have humility is to be open about one's weaknesses and faults. People relate to others when they are willing to see and admit their weaknesses.

In order to establish a helping relationship, Carl Rogers says one must be as honest as possible about self. He calls it "congruence." That is when one's outer expression accurately represents his inward feelings.

To be open means that

1. The outer expressings represent the inner feelings—negative or positive. If angry, one should show it or at least not be deceitful by acting as if he were pleased.
2. One is willing to let others see him as he really is at the moment—whether the picture is good or bad.
3. One does not shock or hurt others with the truth but is dependably real about himself at all times.
4. One is able to be himself and act natural.
5. One is willing to admit his faults first to himself, then to God, and then to some other significant person in his life in order to keep growing in self-knowledge.
6. One knows himself to be accepted by God—with his faults and virtues.
7. One says what he really feels at the moment and not what might be expected under the circumstances.
8. One knows and accepts himself, realizing that divine love makes this possible. He rests in God's grace, not in personal achievements or ability.
9. One is humble. Humility is standing tall as possible in one's own ability "but always against the bigness of God so you never forget how little your bigness really is" (Phillips Brooks). Humility is strength and not weakness because one stands on the rock of truth and his energy is outgoing in creativity; none is needed for defending a false self.

10. One enhances his personal relationships by admitting his humanity.
11. One is willing to be vulnerable in order to glorify God, as was Jesus.

Thought Questions

1. Is it easy to be completely honest about yourself?
2. Do you think most people are humble today?
3. How important is humility for good group discussion leaders?
4. Is real humility "running yourself down"?
5. Where is the scripture that says no one can assist in this work except he shall be humble and full of love?
6. Would there be any value in making a moral inventory occasionally?
7. How could you grow in your honesty about yourself?
8. How could you become more humble?
9. What is the relation between humility and transparency?
10. What did Paul mean when he said that he "came in weakness"?
11. What did God mean when he said to Moroni, "Because thou hast seen thy weakness, thou shalt be made strong" (Ether 5:38)?

4. Empathy

To relate to others one must cultivate a sensitivity to their feelings. It is not enough to know how one feels; he must also care enough to discover how his friends feel. He must "walk in their moccasins" before he passes judgment. Empathy is entering others' lives and feeling what they feel. God came over to humanity's side in Christ in order to communicate His love and win men to Him. A person who loves others will care about their feelings. He will go over to
66

his friends' side in empathy to fully understand and communicate with them. He will try to empathize with them.

Sometimes we offend by remarks which cut deeply and we don't even realize it. The inactive member who is greeted at church with "Look who's here, the roof may fall in!" is not being greeted by a member who has empathy. I have sometimes said half-jokingly we actually run enough people away from our churches by casual statements which offend that if we only kept those coming who drop in . . . at the end of the year our buildings would be full.

Recently a pastor's wife confessed to me her blunder in greeting an inactive woman at church with the question, "Where's your husband?" It was embarrassing the first Sunday to explain his disinterest in religion and preference to fishing. That wasn't too bad but the next three Sundays the same question was asked by a nervous pastor's wife simply trying to make conversation with one she didn't know too well. On the fourth Sunday the wife of the fisherman chose to stay home rather that face the interrogation at the church door. How many people have we offended because we lacked empathy. In small groups we learn how other people feel. We can grow in our ability to empathize with them.

It is reported that J. F. Curtis was a great debater, back in the days of church debates, especially with one particular church. It is said he knew more about their doctrine than they did. The secret of his success was the ability to understand their thinking. This is one secret of effective communication. To empathize with another human being facilitates understanding and communication.

Empathizing means

1. Being sensitive enough in personal relations to detect when one has said or done something the other person interprets as a threat (criticism, judgment, negative evaluation).

2. Realizing it is not what one thinks or feels in the relationship but the other person's interpretation that builds or destroys a relationship.
3. Acting in such a manner that others feel free of criticism or inferiority.
4. Trying to enter into the world of the other person's emotions and feeling what he is experiencing without fear of being trapped or hurt.
5. "Standing in the shoes" of the other person and seeing the world from his point of view.
6. Helping others feel that the locus for evaluation lies within themselves, (one must protect not only his own God-given agency but help others keep theirs). A maturing person is increasingly "inner directed."
7. Not evaluating another person as "good" or "bad" or even judging his actions or comments as "good" or "bad," but giving an opinion concerning one's feelings regarding the matter (not "That was a good sermon," but rather "*I liked* your sermon").
8. Being unafraid of loving others and experiencing what they feel in either pain or joy.
9. Being sensitive enough to others' feelings that one can tell them when they are reacting negatively to what is being said. They may not comment—only keep silent.
10. Remembering that one of the greatest needs of people is to feel free from criticism and rejection. They crave "acceptance." (Care must be taken not to convey the idea that they are not accepted when one is trying to communicate with them.)

Thought Questions

1. Can you tell if you have hurt someone by something you have said?

2. How can you tell the other person's feelings?

3. How important is it in group discussions not to make statements which might offend?

4. What kind of innocent statements can you think of that might tend to offend someone?

5. How can you improve your sensitivity to others?

6. Are you obligated, as a follower of the Christ, to try to understand others—or can you just tell them the gospel story and let it go at that?

7. Do you know anyone you would consider sensitive to people and how they feel? Describe a person who can empathize with others.

5. Potential

In a good relationship others are seen as they might become (under the influence of the Holy Spirit), not what they have been. Sometimes a person's past influences one's feelings too much. Every person has potential and should be seen as what he could become. "Truth is knowledge of things as they are, were, and *are to come*" (Doctrine and Covenants 90:56).

A man who a few years ago answered my letters from a prison cell, is now a deacon in one of our congregations. Someone saw in this man a potential and his past mistakes did not prevent him from changing. God looks upon each of us in light of our possibilities. We are called "saints" because of God's grace—not our past behavior. He believes in us.

When we see others in light of their potential it "sweetens our voice" when we speak to them. Positive vibrations pass between us building friendship and trust. Sometimes a person will make a mistake and want to change but people who cannot forget will not allow him to be different. We must allow people to be different and change by seeing their potential.

A little acorn is a potential oak tree. The truth about the acorn includes its past, present state, but also its potential to become that giant tree. People have great potential regardless of their past. Each person is a potential son of God. Love sees others in light of their potential.

Seeing others in light of their potential means

1. Seeing them (in imagination) as they could become—not as they are now or as they have been in the past.
2. Forgetting their past (if it has been bad).
3. Wanting to see the best in them.
4. Working toward forgiving and forgetting wrongs they have committed.
5. Mentally allowing them to repent and change.
6. Communicating an image of other people so they feel the outlook toward them is positive.
7. Imagining their latent abilities and keeping these in mind as the indicator of their true character (if developed).
8. Seeing them as mature, creative children of God.
9. Having a high regard for all humanity (while admitting man's tendency toward evil).
10. Seeing them as people created in the image of God and possessing certain attributes regardless of the outer shell they present to the world at the moment.

Thought Questions

1. Why is it important in a group discussion to hold a positive view toward all those participating?
2. Do you think the average person sees other people in light of their potential, or do they judge by past deeds?
3. Do you feel it makes a difference how you view others?
4. How can you exercise your imagination creatively

toward others in order to see them as they can become?

5. Do you think God sees us in light of our potential?
6. How can you improve the way you see other people?

6. Challenge to Commitment

All the foregoing principles have been aimed at establishing rapport. There comes a time when the individual must be confronted with the demands of reality and the need for decision and change. This is a crucial point in the relationship but essential if he is to be helped. There are risks but to love fully is to care enough to confront others with the demands of the truths of the gospel.

What is involved in challenging another to commitment? One must

1. Realize that acceptance alone is not sufficient; a person needs a challenge toward the truth (gospel).
2. Plan carefully the timing of this challenge.
3. Seek guidance of the Spirit to know when to make the challenge and in what form.
4. Pray for guidance in how to help most effectively.
5. Cultivate the capacity to follow "inner feelings" in personal relationships.
6. Try to learn when to speak, when to keep quiet, when to press for a decision, and when to leave people alone.
7. Listen prayerfully for guidance for the best approach to particular individuals.
8. Feel the "rhythm of relationships."
9. Help others discover the meaning in their lives as they move to accept the task God is giving them.
10. See the relationship between (1) acceptance of the individual, (2) the need to challenge him, and (3) the need for a period of sustaining fellowship as he works

out his decision to change. Try to "feel" these stages in each individual relationship and learn when to move from one to the other.

11. Learn to wait patiently for inner direction of the Spirit.
12. Move out courageously when divinely guided.
13. Be willing to fail, look foolish, and make mistakes while seeking guidance.
14. Realize that the way to gradually build a capacity to discern guidance is to be willing to respond to impulses, feelings, and "signs."

Thought Questions

1. What is meant by a "sense of timing"?
2. Do you believe men are guided by the Spirit today?
3. Can you recall a time in your life when you felt prompted to talk to someone about a serious matter and you did not? Why did you hesitate to act?
4. Can you recall a time when you spoke too soon?
5. How can you cultivate a capacity to feel the correct timing in relationships?
6. How can you challenge other people to accept the truth (about God, the gospel, themselves)?
7. When you know people are living immorally yet trying to find peace and happiness can you ignore the fact, or must you eventually confront them with the truth and help them see themselves honestly?
8. How can you present the need for repentance to people and still have them feel your acceptance of them as Jesus does?

The foregoing six principles of inter-personal relationships are different components of the great command to love each other. Small group participants need basic understandings of this significant love factor. Good groups will facilitate closer personal relationships and thus create opportunities for the Spirit of God to flow between those in the group.

The needs of the small group leader demand emotional maturity and spiritual insight. They need not frighten anyone away, however. Leaders can grow with their groups. Present group members can become future leaders of other groups. The entire Christian experience is one of rebirth, change, growth, and maturity. Qualified leaders, inspired with a concern for persons, can learn more about interpersonal relationships and move out in effective ministry through small group meetings.

CHAPTER SEVEN

GROUP DYNAMICS

Understanding the dynamics of group process is an essential part of training for small group leadership. Failure is almost an assured result when the emphasis points to methods, materials, or techniques of ministry which fail to take into account the personal interaction of those involved. A growing interest is developing in the area of group dynamics. During the past ten years there has been a flood of writings on this subject, yet the information is still not complete.

In 1947 the Human Dynamics Laboratory was established within the Education Department of the University of Chicago. It was charged to study group operation and eventually to contribute to the theoretical and practical understanding of the effects and control of social-emotional-psychological factors in the classroom learning situation.

In April of 1951 the National Training Laboratory in Group Development made funds available for recruitment and training of observers who would collect observational data on four Basic Training Groups at its summer laboratory.

The Navy assisted in the study of group dynamics through the Group Psychology Branch of the Office of Naval Research. Gradually data is being accumulated in this area. Someone recently estimated the number of books and articles written on the subject in the last ten years to be near 1,400. An article on "Conformity and Commitment" in June 1967 issue of *Transaction,* the magazine for social scientists, is an illustration of the output of new discoveries through research in group dynamics.

Human personality is so complex that scientists will probably never completely understand it, but teachers, counselors, and ministers engaging in group work of various types need the available information.

Modern researchers suggest that the small group discussion method of teaching is the most effective way to influence human behavior. Three common teaching methods are the large lecture, one-to-one instruction, and group discussion. Social scientists have conducted experiments to measure the comparative effectiveness of the various teaching methods, and some significant findings have been reported.

Kurt Lewin, a psychologist at the University of Iowa, reported the results of a study comparing relative effectiveness of lecture versus small group methods made by Red Cross workers during World War II. The experiment was designed to influence housewives to change their cooking methods and menu planning during the war when certain foods were scarce. In spite of good teaching techniques, the lecture method resulted in only 2 percent of the women deciding to change. The small group discussion people covered the same material, ideas, and information, and reported a 32 percent change. This controlled experiment has interesting implications for educational procedures in the world of religion. The church has recently reexamined its teaching methods and philosophy. Dialogue is now considered one of the best approaches. Many churches have already moved toward accommodating the findings of social scientists in their curriculum and educational procedures.

It should be stressed here that the objective is to change human behavior. If teaching is aimed primarily at gathering certain facts and planting them in the heads of students, then the lecture method might on occasions be superior to group discussion. If the aim is to change behavior, group discussion is the best teaching technique.

Another experiment which bears out this fact was conducted by Dana Klurich under the direction of Marian Radke at the State Hospital in Iowa City, Iowa. The objective was to determine the relative effectiveness of the two methods in getting rural mothers to change their habitual ways of feeding babies after leaving the hospital. Exactly the same directions were given to two separate groups, the only difference being the methods of teaching. One was by lecture and the other by group discussion. Tested results two and four weeks after the mothers left the hospital revealed that the discussion group had produced a much higher degree of compliance.

Lewin reports the following conclusions (*Readings in Social Psychology,* New York, Henry Holt & Co., 1947, reprinted in *Selected Readings on the Learning Process,* edited by Harris and Schwahn, New York, Oxford University Press, 1961):

"1. Decisions to change behavior patterns are always more effective in small groups of open discussion than in the lecture method.

"2. Change in behavior in the group discussion method does not depend on the personality of the leader.

"3. Decisions made by the individuals in a group setting are more lasting and possess a greater enduring factor than decisions made individually.

"4. People will change behavior more readily if the group they belong to is changing at the same time. The resistance to change which is part of human nature may be due to the fear of rejection by peers if one departs from old standards. This resistance is removed if the group changes at the same time."

Lewin further reports:

"Perhaps one might expect single individuals to be more pliable than groups of like-minded individuals. However, experiences in leadership training, in changing food habits, work production, criminality, alcoholism, and prejudices all indicate that it is usually easier to change individuals formed into a group than to change any one of them separately. If the group standard itself is changed, the resistance which is due to the relationship between individual and group standard is eliminated."

Something extremely dynamic happens in a group of people when the atmosphere is relaxed, where the leader understands and accepts each person, and where the goal of the meeting is to help everyone grow in spiritual maturity and commitment to Jesus Christ. If the social scientists are correct, this has a direct relationship to teaching methods in the church. To be more effective cottage meetings, church school classes, and all teaching techniques may have to include more discussion. More study and research are needed to relate recent findings of the experts to the particular problems in the church.

Two distinct levels exist in each group meeting—content and feeling. Many small group meetings focus almost entirely on the content level and ignore the dynamic factor of participants' feelings. Both levels need attention by understanding leaders. Group members must feel wanted, needed, and appreciated; above all they need to be listened to. While the content of discussion is very important and should be given serious attention, the feeling level in small groups is more elusive but equally important.

One significant key to the group discussion's success in influencing persons appears to be the factor of involvement.

When group participants are allowed to talk and others listen with interest, something almost magic happens. To learn and change, people have to be "open." Participation in groups has the effect of thawing resistance to change, and new ideas are heard with a greater chance of acceptance. After expressing his own ideas one is more willing to hear others' viewpoints.

Paul Tillich has said, "Communication is a matter of participation. Where there is no participation there is no communication" (*Theology of Culture,* Oxford Press, 1969).

While the amount of material and information presented may be less in group discussion than in the lecture method, the individual may receive and absorb significant information at a deeper level when allowed to participate. Involvement is the key. The warm accepting attitude on the part of all members of the group provides the foundation for the transfer of ideas, concepts, and feelings otherwise never communicated.

Small group work in some areas has fallen into the same trap of group guidance in education. Many educators were pushed to attempt group procedure without sufficient experience in the dynamics of interpersonal relationships. Many negative results came from insensitive leaders, and for a while group guidance fell into low esteem by many educators. This need not happen in the church. There is more foundation for understanding now; however, proper training and exposure must be provided for potential group leaders.

It has now been established by researchers such as Kurt Lewin and Carl Rogers that the group is a very powerful instrument in influencing behavior. People affect the group, but also the group has a great effect on the individuals composing it. Harleigh and Audrey Trecker list ten basic facts discovered in research regarding the influence of the group on the individual.

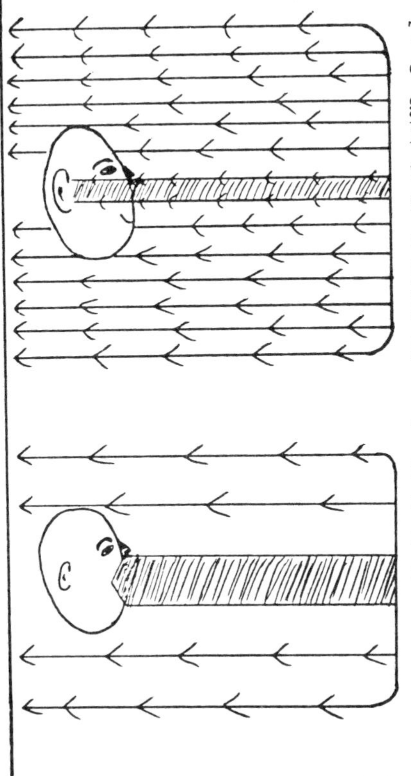

This drawing illustrates the contrast in lecture and group discussion. In the lecture method, information is generally more extensive and better organized. Sometime, however, little is absorbed (dark line). The listener is often passive and uninvolved.

The group discussion method may present less information less well organized, but frequently more is absorbed (dark line) than in the lecture method. When the person talks he is involved and thus becomes more open to new ideas.

"1. Groups influence the way people learn. In fact, everyone learns faster, remembers more, and solves problems better in groups than when working alone.

"2. People get their attitudes, beliefs, and feelings in large part from the groups to which they belong and in which they participate.

"3. Being a part of a group affects the goals of individuals. Group standards are very powerful.

"4. Group experience operates to modify the

individual's habits of living, working, and otherwise carrying out life's pursuits.

"5. Group connections can be thought of as mirrors in that they reflect back a picture of true personality.

"6. Groups provide people with needed help and support. This is especially true in times of stress.

"7. Groups influence choice making in "either or" situations where alternatives are presented.

"8. Groups have a definite effect upon speed, accuracy, and productivity in the work situation.

"9. Groups affect the individual's susceptibility to fear and frustration and his recovery from them is hastened because of the security-giving function of the group.

"10. Groups place limits on natural drives for power and help provide needed control in working out conflicts regarding authority and dependency."—Harleigh B. and Audrey R. Trecker, *How to Work with Groups,* Woman's Press, New York, 1952.

What Makes Up a "Group?" Herbert A. Thelen lists nine characteristics or properties which tend to identify what comprises a group: (1) The membership can be defined. (2) The members think of themselves as constituting a group. (3) There is a sense of shared purpose among them. (4) There is a feeling of greater ease of communication among members than between members and nonmembers. (5) Each member has a sense of approval or disapproval for himself and his actions, receiving feedback from others in the group. (6) He feels an obligation to respond to the behavior of others in the group. (7) He has expectations for certain ways of behaving in various situations in which the group finds itself. (8) There are leadership policies and roles. (9) There emerges a status system, a hierarchy of worth of individuals to the group. In a mature group this is based on demonstrated skills and abilities to contribute to the group (from *Dynamics of Groups at Work,* University of Chicago Press, 1954).

Underneath and behind all group techniques are some basic assumptions or beliefs. This philosophy will determine the practice in the small group meeting. Each group is different and specific practices will vary, but there are some universal principles of effective group dynamics. It is helpful to learn to identify these and use them. Gordon Lippitt and Warren H. Schmidt have listed the following principles common to all effective groups:

"(1) *Any group can become better if it focuses some of its attention on the feelings members have toward one another.* Tension wastes valuable energy, prevents objective examination of proposals presented by certain members, and in general makes the group experience less enjoyable and profitable.

"(2) *Every individual is important and capable of making some contribution to the group.* Mutual trust and respect are given to each member. An atmosphere is created in which everyone feels free to express his ideas.

"(3) *A group has the power to improve its process of operation and its results.* Apathy or internal strife need not hamper any group for an indefinite period.

"(4) *Leadership is more effective if it is shared rather than concentrated.*

"(5) *A group progresses best in an atmosphere of honesty and frankness.* Members may need an occasional "blow-off" in which to get rid of some of their tensions."—*My Group and I,* Arthur C. Croft Publications, New London, Connecticut, 1955.

Examples of the ability to change people are seen in many self-help groups. Overweight persons needing extra strength to diet formed TOPS (Take Off Pounds Sensibly), Weight Watchers, and Overeaters Anonymous. There is a similar group called Recovery, Inc., for persons needing help with mental problems. The Seven-Step Foundation for ex-convicts is group-oriented. Drug addicts, gamblers, and other people in need of behavior change are finding the small group principles applicable to their situations.

The success at Mayo Clinic illustrates to some degree the group idea. "Team diagnosis" is used instead of the old concept of one doctor treating the patient. Another example is presented by Napolean Hill in his book, *Think and Grow Rich*. He says that a basic principle of the successful millionaires in America is the "master mind concept." An industrial leader gathers around him a group to think out together ideas which may help to advance the company's goals. This is all related. Something creative is possible in a group setting when right relationships exist.

Prisoners of World War II and the Korean conflict found the enemy using group method tactics to change loyalties when other types of "brainwashing" failed. Efforts to change the philosophy of prisoners failed in the lecture method and in the one-to-one encounter. However, when small groups of prisoners were assembled and the atmosphere of the discussion was controlled by the leader, a much higher rate of success in changing political ideologies was reported. The small group method can be used effectively for good or evil. The technique itself is amoral or neutral. The point is, it works.

The challenge to the church is to understand the dynamics and utilize them for the advancement of the kingdom of God. Jesus is our best example. He utilized the small group approach with the Twelve because human nature is such that this procedure is the most natural way to train and to transmit faith.

CHAPTER EIGHT

GROUP DISCIPLINES

Discipline and depth are two words that have a significant relationship in small groups. Commonly agreed upon disciplines give the meetings depth and meaning. Recognized leaders in the small group movement stress the importance of the members agreeing on certain disciplines. This vital element cannot be imposed upon an unwilling group but must arise out of common consent.

Thomas Steenlights (*Spiritual Renewal Through Personal Groups*) writes:

> "I seemed possessed with two closely connected ideas: (1) that spiritual freedom and faith could come to a person who shared in a small group dedicated to the search for God's truth, and (2) that joy in religion was to be found in the disciplined life."

Indeed these two ideas are very closely related. Small groups in which lives are being changed and maturity is resulting are those which have a sense of direction born of depth through shared group disciplines.

The number of disciplines and the manner by which each individual carries them out in his daily life varies. The need for clear understanding and commitment, however, is a common thread which runs through all successful groups. Clyde Reid (*Groups Alive-Church Alive*) feels the agreed disciplines are so vital that he suggests the group draw up a contract at the first meeting.

Here is the checklist he suggests:

"1. Purpose of the group:
"2. Meetings: When?__________ How Often?________
    Begin a.m.__________ p.m.__________ Close____
    a.m._______ p.m._______
"3. Proposed size of group: Minimum___ Maximum___
    Composition of group: Open to_______________

____

"4. Level of group interaction:
    _____________________________ business matters
    _____________________________ discussion of ideas
    _____________________________ personal sharing
other_______________________ other___________
"5. Leadership pattern: Leadership of the group will
    reside in ______________________________

____

"6. Group disciplines agreed upon:

____

____

____

____

"7. Other decisions agreed upon:

____

____

____

At the Church of the Savior in Washington, D.C.—an innovative congregation based primarily on small groups—a candidate for membership in the church stands before the congregation and makes the following statement: "Unreservedly and with abandon I, ____________, commit my life and destiny to Christ and promise to give him priority in all the affairs of my life. I will seek first the kingdom of God and his righteousness. Regardless of time, energy, and money, I commit myself to becoming an informed, mature Christian. I give God the throne in my relation to the material things I possess in life. I will seek to bring every phase of my life under the Lordship of Christ." Discipline is the key element following this commitment.

This commitment to Christ involves a relationship to the people. There are many things a person can do alone, but being a Christian is not one of them. The Christian is, above all things, in a state of union with Christ and a union with His followers. The love of His children is inseparable from the love of God.

The discipline of the Church of the Savior is based on the conviction that, in religion as elsewhere, discipline means power. Members of this unique church believe that a group that requires little of its members has little power among them. One person observed, "Real spiritual capacity requires at least as much concentration in training as learning to play a musical instrument. . . ." It is this conviction which motivated the Church of the Savior to establish a minimum discipline. It is assumed that each member will advance as far beyond this as he is able. This minimum discipline calls for the following:

1. Daily prayer
2. Weekly worship
3. Daily study of the scriptures
4. Membership in a fellowship group or participation in the educational program
5. Tithing as a minimum stewardship program
6. Daily expression of Christian love and redeeming service

John Casteel (*Spiritual Renewal Through Personal Groups*) comments that groups often adopt a rule for their daily life as the basis for their common life in the group. Such a rule serves a number of purposes:

1. It assures the study, thought, and prayer of the members to provide the substance of the meeting hour.
2. It gives members the means of working into their own personal lives the insights, truths, and demands they have discovered and shared in the group meeting.
3. It keeps the members steadily at the task of nurturing and disciplining their own individual lives for growth in the life of the Spirit.
4. It serves as a bond between members even while they are separated from one another—especially when an individual finds himself confronted by trouble or temptation or discouragement too great for him to meet with his own resources.

The content of such rules varies according to the needs and interest of the group meeting. Usually the following points are included:

1. *A daily period of personal reading, meditation, and prayer.* This often includes the reading of agreed passages from the Bible and prayer for each member by name as well as for the common concerns of the group as a whole.
2. *Study and nurture.* The group agrees to read a book which is to serve as a basis for discussion or study or some devotional book to strengthen spiritual life.
3. *Faithfulness in attendance at group meetings.* This is at the top of member's calendar priorities (with emphasis on arriving on time).
4. *Faithfulness in participation at public worship in church.*
5. *A discipline of the use of one's time and energies.*

86

Ample margins should be available for the carrying out of the purposes and responsibilities of the life into which the group is moving.

6. *Some reckoning with one's standard of living.* This should assure the responsible use of one's economic means, sometimes expressed in the practice of tithing.

7. *Acceptance of individual responsibility within the group for some kind of outreach and service in the church or community or toward particular persons in need.* The group may not be ready to accept all these rules at the beginning. Whichever ones are adopted should be drawn up by the members themselves and should go only as far as they feel able to obey at their present stage of growth. Above all, it should be remembered that the rule does not exist for its own sake but as a means to help all members of the group realize its fundamental purpose—their growth in love of God and of other people.

The Moravians made wide use of groups and may have influenced Wesley with their possibilities. As Methodism took shape, it consisted of societies which were originally an adjunct to the Church of England. These societies in turn were made up of smaller units referred to by various names. Wesley himself liked the old English word "band" which signified a little company. Some of the rules of the society formulated by Wesley as recorded in his general work follow.

"In obedience to the command of God, by St. James and by the advice of Peter Bohler, it is agreed by us

"1. That we will meet together once a week to confess our faults one to another, and pray one for another, that we may be healed.

"2. That the persons so meeting be divided into

several bands, or little companies, none of them consisting of fewer than five or more than ten persons.

"3. That every one in order speak as freely, plainly, and concisely as he can, the real state of his heart, with his several temptations and deliverances, since the last time of meeting.

"4. That all the bands have a conference at eight every Wednesday evening, begun and ending with singing and prayer.

"5. That any desiring to be admitted into the society be asked, 'What are your reasons for desiring this? Will you be entirely open, using no kind of reserve? Have you any objection to any of our orders?' "—From the *Journal of Rev. John Wesley,* edited by Newer Curnock, Epworth Press, 1938, London.

One interesting movement utilizing disciplines in church renewal has come from the Methodists in Tallahassee, Florida, and is called "Ten Brave Christians." Sam Teague, a banker and former mayor of the capital city, was a Sunday school teacher in a church where nothing was happening. Out of a desire to motivate and help his young adults he prayed. Prompted by the Spirit he posted a notice which read:

"Wanted, Ten Brave Christians for the month of March, 1965

"1. Who will meet once each week to pray together.

"2. Who will give two hours each week to God.

"3. Who will give God one-tenth of earnings in this month.

"4. Who will spend 5:30 to 6:30 each morning in prayer-meditation.

"5. Who will witness his experience with God to others."

A group of people volunteered to follow these disciplines for thirty days, and amazing things began to happen which have resulted in a number of groups of similar nature being started in that church. People have traveled all over the United States sharing their insights and enthusiasm about the program.

Ben Campbell Johnson of the Institute of Church Renewal of Atlanta, Georgia, has developed a Discipline and Discovery Program using some of the Ten Brave Christians' ideas and giving it his own unique twist. Russel Bow says that the keys to church renewal are (1) prayer, (2) discipline, and (3) witness (*Integrity of Church Membership*).

Reverend Bow is convinced that membership is too lightly taken today and he has initiated a program in his church of annually renewing membership vows. He has the congregation take the following Covenant of the Yoke of Christ (Matthew 11:29):

"Recognizing the need for spiritual renewal (Titus 3:5) in my life (Psalm 51:10) and in the church, I hereby renew my vows of membership and seek to open my life to the waiting grace of God by surrendering my will to the way of Christ and undertaking to wear his yoke in the following ways:

"1. *Meeting God Daily* at a set time of prayer and Bible reading (Daniel 6:10 and Acts 3:1, 17:11).

"2. *Weekly Fellowship,* participating both in private worship and meetings of a small group for study, sharing experiences and prayer (Hebrews 10:25).

"3. *Proportionate Giving* of time and money, giving some time each week for service to God through the church and accepting realistically as my goal the tithe as the first reasonable step in Christian giving (Malachi 3:10, Matthew 23:21, and I Corinthians 16:2).

"4. *Seeking to Grow* in love for other Christians and all men everywhere (John 13:35, I John 3:14).

"5. *Witnessing* in my daily life, daily work, and daily words something of what God has done and is doing in my life (Matthew 5:16 and Acts 1:8).

"Realizing I may fail in some of these disciplines, I will seek the help of God and my fellow Christians in living by this covenant. My signature is affixed in an effort to strengthen my own decision for a new life in Christ."—*Integrity of Church Membership,* pages 68-69.

Another famous small group is called the Yoke-fellow Fellowship. "The Order of the Yoke," as it is now developing, exists to help people be more effective members of their religious organizations. Their minimum discipline reads,

"As one who seeks to submit his will to the will of Christ, I humbly undertake to wear his yoke in the following ways:

"1. *The Discipline of Prayer.* To pray every day, preferably at the beginning of the day.

"2. *The Discipline of Scriptures.* To read reverently and thoughtfully every day a portion of Scripture, following a definite plan.

"3. *The Discipline of Worship.* To share once each week in the public worship of God.

"4. *The Discipline of Money.* To give a definite portion of my annual income to the promotion of the Christian cause.

"5. *The Discipline of Work.* To strive to make my daily work a Christian vocation.

"6. *The Discipline of Study.* To develop my mental powers by careful reading and study."—Helen Shoemaker, *Power by Prayer Groups,* Revell Company, page 103.

Another example of a rule of life is a card entitled: "A rule of life for Christians" which was prepared for the members of Calvary Episcopal Church in New York City when Samuel Shoemaker was rector. The disiplines are as follows:

"1. *A Definite Commitment to Jesus Christ* made at sometime once and for all and renewed each time I pray.

"2. *A Definite Time with Him Each Day,* if possible at the start of the day, consisting of Bible study, prayer, and meditation.

"3. *Weekly Fellowship* with other Christians, in the church and in a smaller company for mutual help.

"4. *A "Tithe" Gift* [one-tenth] of my income to God's work in the world.

"5. *An Honest Effort* day by day to apply in my work and human relations Christian love, humility, truth, and faith.

"6. *A Real Effort by Life and by Witness* to win others to him, his way of life, and his kingdom. I will try, with God's help, to live up to this rule of life and put it where it will remind me daily of my promises to him."–Helen Shoemaker, *Power by Prayer Groups,* pages 103-104.

The Disciplined Order of Christ under the leadership of Albert E. Day has the following six duties for its members:

"1. *To seek for ourselves* the highest New Testament standard of Christian experience in life.

"2. *To seek to promote* the highest New Testament standards of Christian experience in life among others.

"3. *To seek first the kingdom of God,* not in our lives merely but in the life of the world.

"4. *To acknowledge the praying and witnessing church*, wherever it exists in the body of Christ.

"5. *To be guided in the meaningful fulfillment* of these duties by the recognition of the validity and authority of centuries of Christian experience, especially with their universal testimony.

"6. *To support and advance the discipline order of Christ* by earnest prayer and an annual sacrificial gift."

The Kirkridge Fellowship is a Christian Group near Bankof, Pennsylvania. Its disciplines include the following:

"1. To keep a daily one-fourth hour devotion before nine a.m. (or at another hour).

"2. To read the agreed lectionary and use the agreed hymns.

"3. To pray at the day's end.

"4. To offer grace at each meal.

"5. To make the personal retreat each month.

"6. To tithe consistently.

"7. To work for the growth of the Christian cell where I am.

"8. To share corporate church worship weekly and interchurch activity quarterly.

"9. To make a retreat with other Kirkridge members once yearly."

The lectionary mentioned in rule two includes the reading of the same Bible chapter each day for a week, and the memorization of one hymn each month. In addition to these rules there are eight intentions:

"1. To live frugally.

"2. To identify myself with all those with whom Christ would have fellowship.

"3. To demonstrate my Christianity in civic action.

"4. To grow intellectually as a Christian.

"5. To practice Christian reconciliation.

"6. To share myself with my household.

"7. To share my Christian experience with some new person monthly.

"8. To pray constantly."

Guideposts Magazine (February 1962) carried nine disciplines of the major religions of the world indicating how universal the need for discipline is.

"Here are nine practices followed in varying degrees by members of Christian-Judeo faiths. How many are a part of your life? If your score is low, try working out a plan over a period of months whereby you gradually strengthen your religious life.

"1. A surrendering of your life to God (which means that everything you do becomes an instrument for his purpose).

"2. A daily period of personal prayer, a meditation, a reading of God's word from the Bible, and a study of other religious literature.

"3. Regular family devotions at home, with all members taking some active part.

"4. Regular sacrificial giving to God's work a definite portion of your time, income, and other resources.

"5. Weekly worship in church (or synagogue).

"6. Gathering regularly with other committed people to form a small group which meets in the home, office, church, or some other place for spiritual fellowship and team prayer.

"7. The determination to apply your religious principles to all your responsibilities at your place of work.

"8. A prayerful desire to bring to other people through the quality of your living and through spoken witness the revelation of God's love so that others may also seek to find and serve Him.

"9. Participation at least once a year in a religious retreat or conference which emphasizes meditation and self-discipline."

One wonders if Zion will be built with anything less.

The Spiritual Growth Groups formed in Tulsa developed the following points of discipline:

"I promise for thirty days to

1. Attend four weekly meetings

2. Read a scripture assignment daily (one-half chapter from the Gospel of Mark or other selected scripture which the group agrees upon).

3. Pray daily at a set time for everyone in the group and myself.

4. Attend church worship services at least once each week.

5. Fast from one meal on the day of the group meeting."

The Spiritual Growth Group meetings consist of silence, shared insights from assigned scripture reading, discussion of personal needs and struggles to follow Christ, and prayer.

The purpose of the Spiritual Growth Groups was to grow in the following areas:

1. Know who Jesus really is.
2. Make a genuine commitment to him.
3. Relate this commitment to daily life.
4. Share this new life with other persons.
5. Get involved in helping to bring Christ's kingdom on earth.

94

After the four weeks experiment group members were to evaluate the experience, pray for guidance, and do as they felt about continuing to meet. Then they were to report discoveries as a result of the experiment.

In Houston, Texas, an Episcopal Church has the following disciplines for church members:

"To glorify God, to strengthen the church, to help the world, to grow in my Christian life, in the name of Jesus Christ our Lord, as an expression of my love for God, I will do my best to

1. Seek God's plan through a daily time of listening prayer and Bible reading.

2. Worship weekly in the church (with emphasis on the monthly Holy Communion).

3. Participate regularly in a weekly group for Christian sharing, study, and prayer.

4. Give regularly a definite share of my income to spread God's kingdom through the church and in the world."

"And, as an expression of love for my neighbor, I will do my best to

5. Pray daily for others with thanksgiving.

6. Exercise faithfully the particular ministries to which God calls me in the fellowship of the church and in the world.

7. Speak and act so that my daily life is a witness to the love of God in Christ as I have come to know it. So help me God."—Claxton Monro and William S. Taegel, *Witnessing Laymen Make Living Churches*, Word Books, page 78.

It is obvious that one thing effective small groups have in common is their emphasis on discipline. Any beginning group will want to carefully consider the need to adopt minimum disciplines for those participating. These disciplines often will open doors for spiritual growth. To avoid the disciplines is to invite shallowness and mediocrity in the group. Many groups which have failed have had no disciplines (or little agreed upon ones).

During the last ten years, while being involved in various forms of small group meetings in two districts in Oklahoma, I have become convinced that we have been too hesitant to ask our groups to accept disciplines. The conviction is growing that as leaders we must be more daring and perhaps even more committed ourselves to these disciplines; then we will be better prepared to ask others to accept them. No doubt the power available to the church—promised in scripture and referred to often as the "endowment"—will come when people are willing to accept the disciplines required for such blessings. Small groups may be the beginning of preparation for this endowment.

CHAPTER NINE

LEADERSHIP

Effective small groups are dependent on good leadership. Leaders can be ministers, unordained men, women, or youth. Any church member can lead a small discussion group.

Characteristics of good group leaders include

1. Love of people
2. Humility
3. Desire to grow with others
4. Testimony of Christ and his church
5. Ability to relate to people
6. Desire to witness
7. Ability to adjust to circumstances (flexibility)
8. Emotional maturity and stability
9. Willingness to admit error and learn from mistakes
10. Dependence on prayer

Few people will possess all these qualities. However, it is often surprising who makes a good leader, so no one should be ruled out entirely.

Group leaders do not have to be outstanding in the usual sense of leadership (dynamic, or unusually knowledgeable). Some persons seem to have the sensitivity to lead groups almost by nature, but most have to learn through training. Everyone who truly wants to can increase his skill and effectiveness.

A common failing is the tendency to "overlead." The one in charge might well be called a facilitator—or convener. The stereotyped leader who knows all and dominates is an image to be avoided.

The Gospel

The effective small group leader should have some knowledge of the gospel, a testimony of Jesus Christ, and something to share in the group meetings. He (or she) should consider these questions before accepting the role of leader.

(1) Do I really know who Jesus Christ is?
(2) Have I made a serious commitment of my life to him?
(3) Can I relate my commitment to my daily life situations?
(4) Can I relate my experience of conversion to another human being?

During the progress of the meetings the leader will be aware of these questions and gently move the participants to consider them at some point, even though not one of these points may ever be the specific topic for a given meeting. They will aid the group in evaluating its progress.

It is helpful if the leader understands something of the conversion process. Characteristics of the "pagan" life-style and the Christian way are different at key points. Good groups help move persons toward a positive change.

Characteristics of the Old Life	*Characteristics of the New Life in Christ*
1. Man (self) the central figure	1. Christ the central figure
2. Pride, self-sufficiency, inability to see own faults, fear of weakness	2. Dawning humility, awareness of limitations, confession of faults, and openness
3. Uncommitted to any cause (self-centered)	3. Genuine commitment to Christ and the fellowship (church)
4. Guilt, anxiety	4. Inner peace, experience of forgiveness, release, joy

98

5. Boredom, lack of purpose	5. Rising urgency to discover and fulfill one's mission in life (sense of great purpose in God's kingdom)
6. Aloofness, go-it-alone, independent spirit	6. Humble dependence on the fellowship of the Saints, acknowledging need for love
7. Refusal to acknowledge the needs of others, apathy	7. Growing compassion for others, empathy, caring
8. Selfish with possessions, irresponsible, compulsive, spender, wasteful	8. Recognition of God's ownership and own stewardship, accountable
9. Ineffective personal relationships, continually misunderstanding people, hurt feelings, contention	9. A growing ability to get along successfully, joyously with others.
10. Inability to witness to anyone significantly, failure to relate to persons at depth level	10. Growing ability to help others find God and come into the kingdom way of life; effective witness

Everyone has characteristics on both sides of this chart. The Saint is a serious Christian who is in the process of moving from the old to the new life. Essentially, he is one who has Christ abiding in him. He has had some type experience or confrontation with God and has made a decision to covenant with Christ in a new life relationship. This experience most generally occurs in a social setting involving relationships with other people who have already had some experience with God. That is why small groups can be so effective in spreading the gospel. The leader who is sensitive to all this can be a tremendous help in promoting the climate for conversion.

A good leader will ask himself (or herself) some key questions such as: What happens to one who is under conviction? What attitudes are present in the unrepentant? What attitudes represent a change toward the kingdom? Can I detect someone responding to the Spirit?

A group leader ought to be sensitive to the movement of the Holy Spirit in the lives of members of the group. Many times this is demonstrated by an individual changing some behavior or attitudes.

Human Behavior

An understanding of human nature, as well as a knowledge of the gospel, is a prerequisite of leadership. Jesus commanded that we feed his sheep (John 21:16). We must be rather familiar with two things to accomplish this: We should know the "feed" (Christ, his gospel message, gifts, power), and we should know the "sheep" (people, their needs, feelings). For a long time we seem to have laid emphasis on the necessity of knowing the gospel. Equally as important is an understanding of people. If we listen to any good fisherman we'll quickly learn how well informed he has become on the habits of fish. He not only knows his tackle and bait but he understands what time of year the fish are attracted to certain types of lures. Any successful fisher-of-man must take time to study people, seek deeper insights into human nature, know the mood of the times, discover the present fears and desires of people, and decide what it will take to reach them. If we love Christ and want to win men to him we will pay the price to learn these essentials.

One of the growing areas of study in recent years is the field of interpersonal relationships. The dynamics of group work and the interplay between personalities is fascinating. To minister to people we ought to have at least some elementary knowledge of group dynamics and personal relationships. What is the feeling of the other person we want to help? Do we really know very much about humanity? Can

100

we help people significantly without understanding them?

Any attempt to help others must be done within some frame of reference regarding the nature of man. From this we establish a philosophy for a method of ministry. For example, if we do not believe in the agency of man we shall tend toward a method where force and pressure techniques are dominant tools in ministry. This probably would not be successful in small groups. If, however, our philosophy regarding man includes the precious gift of individual freedom, our entire approach is different. With this latter view we are inclined toward methods of friendly persuasion and loving influence; strong-arm tactics are out of place.

Seven Considerations of the Nature of Persons

1. *Every human being is a unique individual of great worth.*

"The worth of souls is great in the sight of God" (Doctrine and Covenants 16:30). The gospel is the good news of God's great concern over every person in His universe. The lost sheep parable and many other illustrations from the ministry of Jesus convey this profound truth. People are "ends," not "means." People do not exist to fill pews or support a branch budget; rather, as persons made in the image of God, they are unique and of profound worth within themselves. The church and all its ministries exist to support and assist individuals.

One way leaders can acknowledge a person's worth is to acknowledge and accept that person's "uniqueness" and allow him to be himself. Agency—a concept very dear to Saints—means allowing another person the freedom to be himself. A very wise man recently said, "The problem of our age is to allow each person to truly be himself."

God has fashioned his universe on uniqueness. No two snowflakes are the same. No two blades of grass are identical.

No two grains of sand are shaped exactly alike. No wonder then that God would make men, his highest creation, so different. Individual uniqueness must be respected; no one should violate another's agency by trying to change him into some predetermined mold or image.

In the prodigal son parable the father *let* his son go away. Though he had desires for his son's behavior, he was waiting at the door longing for the prodigal's return. Just as he *let the boy go away,* Saints today must allow people their agency.

Each person should be encouraged in his uniqueness. Much strife is born of competition—persons seeking to outshine one another. The gospel releases people from unhealthy competition (not all competition need be unhealthy) and announces to each the good news of every person's singularity. The Christian changes his emphasis from competing with others to a concentration on developing his own and others' abilities.

In a small group meeting the leader must be able to accept each person's uniqueness and should seek to establish an atmosphere of acceptance within the group.

2. *Every human being has great potential.*

Another consideration regarding human nature is the view that every person, regardless of his present apparent abilities or skills has tremendous potential. Experts estimate that the average man uses only 5 to 10 percent of his native ability.

Good leaders will look upon all members of the group in light of their potential and not be limited by their present or past records of behavior. In latter-day revelation God says, "Truth is knowledge of things as they *are, and as they were, and as they are to come*" (Doctrine and Covenants 90:4b). The truth about an acorn includes its potential to become an oak tree.

102

A few years ago I corresponded with a young church man in prison. Today he serves in the priesthood. God saw his potential, and local leaders did not hold his past against him. Many people would never be assigned responsibility if they were considered on the basis of their past performance.

3. *Every human being can change.*

Satan must have invented the phrase, "You can't change human nature." The fact is, everyone changes continually. With understanding, groups may help facilitate a positive change in people.

All ministry, teaching, and social reform are built on the premise that people can change. No matter how frustrating it may be to work with someone who appears to resist change no one should ever succumb to the belief that change is impossible.

Jesus offers people such a radical change in their lives that it is like being reborn and starting life on a different basis. Paul says that if men are in Christ, they are entirely new creatures.

Group leaders will keep open-minded toward every participant and never give up on the possibility of a positive change occurring.

4. *Human beings resist change tenaciously.*

It seems to be human nature to resist change. Some persons resist it more than others. For group leaders this is a fact to be clearly aware of.

Before anyone begins to change deliberately he has to go through a period of "unfreezing" at his present level, usually becoming very dissatisfied and desiring something better. This may accompany a crisis of some sort, or it may come gradually by simple exposure to people who seem to have a better way. The awareness of a need for change may come through contrast between oneself and other (happy) people in the group who live by a different life-style.

Leaders need to understand what factors tend to magnify one's resistance to change and what situations help to reduce the amount of resistance.

5. *Human beings tend to make positive changes in a nonthreatening atmosphere of warm acceptance and honesty.*

Love and friendship appear to be vital elements providing the dynamics for positive change. The love of God revealed in Christ is the supreme motivation for conversion. This same love can be communicated to a lesser degree by individuals in a group where people are able to accept each other. A nonthreatening atmosphere is essential.

A large part of ministry to people is accepting them as they are now so they become free to be themselves and move toward maturity in the gospel. People are not free to change some things about themselves until they feel accepted.

Actually nobody can ever "change" another person; one can act only as an agent of change. The other person always has to decide within himself whether to change or not. Perhaps the greatest contribution is an atmosphere conducive to change—a climate characterized by love, acceptance, honesty, reality, and accountability.

While one feels freer to change in a climate of loving acceptance, at the same time it is essential for group members to be honest about sins, faults, weaknesses, and the need to grow. There can be no illusions about the destructive nature of sin. This combination of acceptance and honesty about immaturity is fertile ground for soul growth.

6. *Gospel truths are often attractive to maturing, nondefensive, unthreatened persons.*

The gospel should not be defensively presented in small groups. It is attractive within itself when shared in love. We
104

do not "sell" the gospel—we only share the good news we have heard. If we try too hard to convince others we may betray our fear that the gospel is not really good news . . . and it won't be accepted. A fanatic is unsure of himself and his product.

It is a relief to realize we do not convert anyone; God does. Our calling is to be channels of the Holy Spirit. We are to remove the barriers to communication and let people see the Christ and the good news in our fellowship. The prime mission of the small group is to expose people to the gospel in loving action.

In the ideal situation there is freedom for all to share convictions, beliefs, ideas, and opinions. Many new thoughts will "float" around in a room where a lively small group is in session. When defensive barriers are eliminated people are free to accept the truths they hear expressed.

A classic example of this occurred in one of the early small group meetings in Tulsa, Oklahoma. A nonmember husband reacted violently against the idea of baptism's being essential in conversion, and he especially objected to immersion. After his vigorous statement silence ensued. Then I asked if he had any other feelings on the subject. No one argued with him. Someone spoke up and shared his baptismal experience. Another quoted from Romans 6, "We are buried with him in baptism."

The conversation changed easily to another subject, and the meeting closed with prayer. The next week the meeting was on another topic, but the subject of baptism eventually came up. The nonmember surprised everyone as he began arguing for immersion as the correct method of baptism. Because no one forced him into a defensive position the week before, he was free to move toward a new viewpoint which he found attractive in the previous discussion.

Truth will sell itself. It only needs exposure with a

minimum of barriers so its impact can be felt. Often proselyters try too hard. God draws men with love.

7. One's view of himself is a significant clue to his capacity for helping others.

A group leader or any person involved in ministry will be greatly affected by his own self concept. The way he feels toward himself will determine his approach to others. Unless he can accept himself as a unique individual, realizing his own strengths and weaknesses, he very likely will not be able to accept other people and allow them their individuality.

A group leader should see himself as a repentant sinner, forgiven by a merciful heavenly Father, loved by Christ, needed in His kingdom, and moving toward fulfilling his unique mission in life. He will be aware of his own need to grow. He will be able to identify his "growing edge" as he progresses toward a healthy self-discovery. He will know himself and be at peace, accepting himself on the basis of repentance and Christ's justification, not his own merits.

A good leader will attempt to keep close contact with Christ and the people.

Group Process

The third category a leader needs to understand is the group process (this will be dealt with in a separate chapter). Briefly, a leader of the small group must not stand out as an authority figure. He should try to facilitate and guide the meeting so that a climate of freedom and sincerity exists. He needs to be an emotionally mature person who does not have to do all the talking or feel he knows all the answers. (One of the greatest faults of most untrained leaders is that they talk too much.) He should be able to confess his own faults and be natural in order to set the climate for others.

The small group leader must pray, and he must love

106

people deeply. He must be sensitive to both the movement of the Spirit of God in the meeting and the feelings of the persons in the group. He needs to be sensitive enough to know when others feel threatened by a statement or when they are experiencing the Spirit of God moving in their lives.

The leader must return questions to the group which are directed to him. After everyone else has had an opportunity to talk and express an opinion, he may speak his own ideas. (This appears to be most difficult for some ministers.) He will need to ask questions to which others will respond. Sometimes he will have to "wait them out." Usually after the group is a few weeks old this is no problem. Silence is helpful. Things can be happening even when no one is talking. Often the leader will need to rephrase a question so people can "get hold of it."

The leader must have a love for people that is expressed in patience, tolerance, courteous listening, and genuine concern. He sets the tone for the entire meeting.

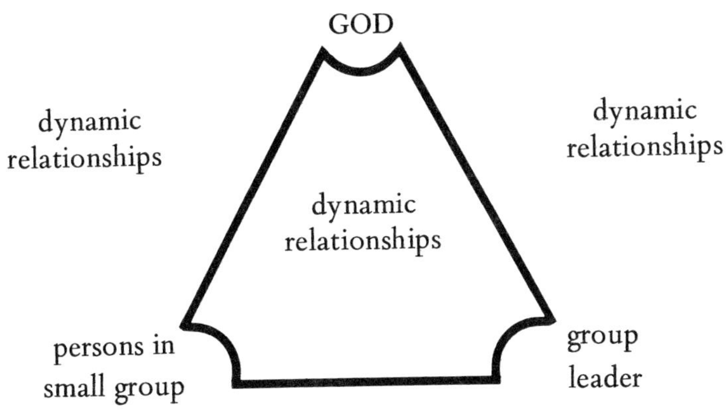

Carl Rogers identified characteristics of a "helping relationship" which have a bearing on the leadership needs for small groups. The leader must establish a certain quality relationship with those to whom he seeks to give ministry. Generally ministers emphasize the relationship to God as being very important but sometimes neglect the importance of establishing a good relationship with others.

The leader's task is to help other men find a personal relationship with God. To do this he must understand people. He must study their feelings, needs, reactions, and hopes.

Ben Franklin expressed his ideas on "How to Communicate" (quoted in a *Herald* article by William Pitt, February 15, 1963):

> "I made it a rule to forbear all direct contradiction to the sentiments of others, and all positive assertion of my own. I even forbid myself . . . to use expressions that imported a fixed opinion, such as certainly, undoubtedly, etc.; and I adopted instead of them, I conceive, I apprehend, or I imagine a thing to be so; or it so appears to me at present. When another asserted something that I thought an error, I denied myself the pleasure of contradicting him abruptly and of showing immediately some absurdity in his proposition: and in answering I began by observing that in certain cases or circumstances his opinion would be right, but in the present case there appeared or seemed to me some difference, etc.

> "I soon found the advantage of this change in my manner; the conversations I engaged in went on more pleasantly. The modest way in which I proposed my opinions procured them a readier reception and less contradiction; I had less mortification when I was found to be in the wrong, and I more easily prevailed with others to give up their mistakes and join with me when I happened to be in the right. And this mode, which I at

first put on with some violence to natural inclination,
became at length so easy, and so habitual to me, that
perhaps for these fifty years past no one has ever heard
a dogmatical expression escape me. And to this habit I
think it principally owing that I had early so much
weight with my fellow citizens when I proposed new
institutions, or alterations in the old and so much
influence in public councils when I became a member;
for I was a bad speaker, never eloquent . . . and yet
generally carried my points."

Do's and Don't's for Group Leaders

DO:
1. Pray for the meeting and all participants.
2. Prepare ahead of time (read assigned scriptures, prepare some good questions, and depend on God for
   guidance).
3. Help all participants feel wanted, appreciated, and
   needed.
4. Listen intently to each person.
5. Look at people while they are talking.
6. Lead the discussion by asking questions.
7. Start on time and end on time.
8. Bring extra books of scripture for those who forget to
   bring their own.
9. Evaluate each meeting and think of ways to improve
   the next one.
10. Relate the group to the congregation.
11. Encourage the spirit of outreach; bring others into the
    group (then divide).
12. Keep Christ in the center of the group meetings.

1. Evaluate each person's statement; let it remain as stated.
2. Interrupt a speaker.
3. Probe deeper (wait for volunteer information).
4. Give advice to anyone in the group—just share.
5. Judge, criticize, or praise unduly.
6. Talk too much—just facilitate discussion.
7. Allow one person to dominate the meeting.
8. Allow a clique spirit to develop.
9. Allow negative criticisms of those outside the group or other churches, races, or politics.
10. Let meeting drift too far away from the central topic.
11. Forget to keep the pastor informed.
12. Lead all the meetings (rotate leadership after the group is stabilized and functioning well).

Leadership Suggestions of One Group in Oklahoma

1. After a few meetings, rotate discussion leadership but maintain a coordinating leader.
2. Set specific goals and disciplines agreed upon by the group.
3. Prepare before meeting (by leader and participants).
4. Hold a weekly meeting of the leader with others in the group for evaluation and planning.
5. Relate topics to specific needs of the group.
6. Report regularly to the pastor.
7. Use conversational prayer in the meeting (to open or close or both).
8. Have a personal question for sharing feelings in the early phase of the meeting (such as "If the door opened and someone brought you the best possible news, what would it be?").

9. Keep a diary of meetings, attendance, and discussion topics.
10. Notify all participants of the exact time and place of meetings.
11. Periodically conduct one meeting to evaluate the group in light of agreed upon goals at the first session.
12. Provide for small children ahead of time (if there are enough to distract the parents during the meeting).
13. Close by inviting the small children to be included in the final prayer.
14. Make a note of follow-up needs of individuals.
15. Pray, pray, pray.

Items for Leaders to Consider

1. How to set up a meeting
   a. Whom to invite
   b. How many to invite
   c. How to extend invitations
   d. Where to hold the meeting
   e. How to get people to the meeting
   f. How to get a compatible group
   g. What to do with children

2. How to open a meeting
   a. What type of refreshments
   b. When to serve refreshments
   c. What seating arrangement
   d. How to get early arrivals to relax
   e. How to get the meeting started
   f. How to build an atmosphere of freedom and naturalness
   g. How to get the discussion going
   h. How to select a topic
   i. How to arrange for regular meeting place, time, etc.

3. How to keep meetings alive
   a. Why some meetings die
   b. Essential elements in a successful meeting
   c. Factors which cause embarrassment and negative reactions
   d. How to make people want to keep coming back
   e. Evaluation by leaders after the meeting
   f. Length of meeting
   g. Starting on time
   h. What versions of the scriptures to use
   i. New people joining the group

4. How to close a meeting
   a. What time to close
   b. Watching the clock
   c. How to close discussion and go into the prayer period
   d. Determining type of prayer to be used
   e. Leading the group in prayer
   f. Saying good-night after the prayer
   g. Helping the hostess with physical rearrangements
   h. Evaluation after the meeting (with whom)

5. How to integrate the small group into the congregational program
   a. Whom to keep informed as to progress of the meeting
   b. How to invite group participants to church services
   c. How to single out individuals for home visits and personal ministry
   d. How to suggest slides or other doctrinal topics to individuals
   e. How to integrate group meetings into a regular visiting program

6. How to use small group method for other purposes within the congregation
   a. How to apply to home ministry
   b. How priesthood can use for spiritual growth
   c. How family units can use
   d. How church school and other departments can use the method

CHAPTER TEN

STARTING A GROUP

Small groups really cannot be routinely "organized." The best groups originate when some individual feels a particular need. Some "pull" or spiritual guidance should precede organization. Motivation is a key factor in the success of a small group meeting. If you are considering forming a group, first ask yourself:

1. Why do I want to start a group?
2. Do I feel superior and want to reach down and help some other person who needs what I think I have?
3. Would I like to discover, *with* other people, a deeper spiritual life?

The next important step is to read materials relative to small group meetings and become familiar with techniques. There are many helpful pamphlets and books on the subject. (A list appears at the back of this book.)

Then you will need to decide whether you want to start small and expand or start big and "let it shake down." An approach to the friends you feel led to invite to the first meeting might be: "I want to find out more about God and myself. I need a few friends with whom I can be honest in my search. Will you join me?" Gradually you locate other interested persons who want to grow in their understanding of God and self. Many people sense the need . . . but don't be surprised if some react cautiously at the beginning.

Set a time and place, then extend invitations to those you'd like to have join you. A little folder entitled, "What is a small group meeting?" (available from the President of

Seventies office, the Auditorium) can be used as an invitational folder and also a teaching device to establish the ground rules on the first night. The folder includes the description of what a small meeting is, why it is being held, who is sponsoring it, and twelve characteristics of a good group discussion.

Select a meeting place where you will have privacy and reasonable comfort. Arrange chairs in a close circle so people can see and hear one another easily. The diameter of the circle should not be over ten feet. Closeness facilitates conversation.

Scriptures should be available for all present. Holding scriptures in hand helps people to feel more involved. You may want to serve light refreshments. A simple drink works best if you are going to rotate the meeting place among the participants. This prevents the tendency of hostesses to compete with one another. As the participants arrive, make sure each one is introduced immediately. Do this in a friendly, natural, relaxed way. Help everyone to feel at ease.

The first phase of the meeting is personal. Following a brief prayer asking for God's presence and blessings, you move through the first phase. Follow this with such icebreakers as "Tell us your name and where you were born" or "Tell us something about yourself so we'll know you better." Vary the questions each week.

Listen to what is said in the group. Help everyone develop a mutual sense of trust. Look at people when they speak. Be interested. In the early meetings it is best to sidestep controversy and deal with personal needs and feelings. Unanswerable questions or theological arguments should not be introduced until the group has developed rapport and stability.

Generally the next phase of the meeting is devoted to some scripture or topic preselected or arising out of the group needs at the moment. The question should be related to life—serious, and worthy of discussion. The group needs to be intentionally going somewhere. One method is to read a Bible passage (preferably a parable or familiar scripture) and ask questions such as

1. What does this passage reveal about God?
2. What does it reveal about me?
3. What is God telling me here about the next step for my life?
4. What is God asking me to be and do for others?

Some groups have found it helpful to have pencil and paper available so they can rewrite the scripture in their own words and then make application to their own lives. Lyman Coleman (see page 187) has produced some very good material to help at this point.

As the discussion progresses, try to keep it personal and experiential. Many groups tend to become theoretical in their approach. If the discussion is kept personal the meeting will be more interesting and meaningful. If someone gets too abstract it may help to say, "Can you give a personal example of what you are saying?" The meeting will have two levels—content and feeling. Both need attention for balance. The feeling level is more subtle and easily overlooked, but it is very vital.

"Faith at Work" has a handbook, *How to Start a Group,* which lists the following helpful hints:

1. A light touch may help you to keep your first group meeting from getting bogged down. Avoid being too serious, ponderous, or grim. Enjoy each other. But if a joke is told which confuses or changes the direction of the conversation, don't be afraid to get it back on the track.

2. Trying to accomplish too much may be a mistake. Give yourself and the others a chance to "feel out" the situa-

tion—to become free and open with each other. Some groups take months, even years, to develop trust and form the deeper relations in life. Be patient.

3. Some awkwardness and reticence may accompany the first meeting. Don't worry about it. Those who are ready for the group experiment will stick to it—the relaxation will come in good time.

4. Time and concern shared between meetings will make the difference between a vital group and an ordinary one (disciplines each day).

5. At the close of the meeting ask, "Where do we go from here? Should an agenda be drawn for the next meeting?"

This handbook and several other similar ones can be ordered for 25c each from Faith at Work, 1000 Century Plaza, Suite 210, Columbia, Maryland 21043.

The following suggestions may prove helpful also:

1. Discuss the Method, Objectives, and Approach at the first meeting. Explain that all ideas are welcome and everyone is to feel free to express himself. At this original gathering the group should decide on the place and time of future meetings, subjects to discuss, disciplines between meetings, and other details—especially the purpose of the group. Freedom in the planning is important. The leader may suggest, but decisions must be made by the total group in common consent.

2. Set an unthreatening tone from the beginning by stating that no one has the final answers. A good slogan is "No one can be wrong in these meetings; all opinions are O.K." Tell the participants to refrain from making dogmatic statements they'll feel obligated to defend, but to feel free to offer ideas as their personal opinions. Some leaders ask their groups to put all the ideas and opinions "out in the middle of the floor" for everyone to see, allowing each participant the freedom to select those ideas appealing to him and reject the

118

others. Freedom of expression should be established at the start. It is not harmful for different opinions to be stated; in fact, it often can be stimulating and helpful. However, it can be a special challenge to the leader to maintain a good spirit throughout the discussion. Humor can help relieve tension so that no one feels threatened. Often by restating an opinion the leader can resolve differences.

3. Feel the rhythm and "flow" of the meeting. Some leaders like to start out with the first of several well-formulated questions before going to the assigned scripture. Open-ended questions are best (such as "What do you think God is like?") Do not ask "yes" or "no" or obvious questions. After a few minutes of good discussion go to the scripture for added help. Discuss its meaning in light of the topic under consideration. Use questions to guide the meeting.

4. Keep conversation personal. This is one of the leader's most difficult tasks, but it is the key to good meetings.

In *Open Circle* (November 1968) Ray Wedaa says that leaders must start with these questions:

"1. What are our motives? If we want to start a group simply because we think other people need it, something is wrong. We have only one legitimate reason for starting and that is because we ourselves need it. We all need to be loved and to have the opportunity to love others, and what better way can this happen than in a small group? I've discovered that God loves me in a very meaningful way through other people.

"2. Are we willing to lead from our own weakness? The only real thing that we have to give to others—aside from God—is ourselves. Are we willing to share our failures, and how God has taught us and loved us through them?

"3. Are we willing to fail? The only people who don't fail are those who don't attempt anything. We must begin with people where they are. Groups, to be real, must center around people's needs. As we change, our needs change, and so there need to be different kinds of groups. A group does not have to last forever, and sometimes it should disband. We ought not to look at ourselves as failures because a group comes to an end. However, if we do fail and can face this, then we are growing.

"4. Are we person-centered—and Christ-centered? All of us need forgiveness on a daily basis. I've discovered in my own life that sharing my struggle or my problem with another person and asking for his prayers gives me a deeper feeling of God's forgiveness than if I try to find it just between God and me."

—Reprinted by permission from *Faith at Work*
1000 Century Plaza, Columbia, Maryland 21043.

Many good groups start with only a few people. It's much easier to be honest with one or two than with twelve or fifteen.

One of the greatest times of challenge and opportunity in a group is when conflict comes. There are bound to be differences and misunderstandings. If you can face these honestly, you can experience real forgiveness, love, and growth.

Don't start a small group without your pastor's approval. When you have teamwork God honors it in miraculous ways.

An excellent formula for a small group meeting was outlined at the Quorums of Seventy meeting at Camp Chihowa near Lawrence, Kansas, in April 1972 by Ben Campbell Johnson, director of the Institute of Church Renewal, Atlanta, Georgia. He led groups of eight in a devotional exercise based on consideration of Matthew 17:14-21 using the following steps:

1. Share personal data to get acquainted
2. Pray.
3. Read the scripture passage through.
4. Reread the passage, underlining the characters in the story.
5. Meditate on the story and empathize in imagination with each character. Feel what each of the following people felt:

   a. The father of the epileptic
   b. The epileptic son
   c. The disciples who could not heal
   d. Jesus
   e. The crowd

6. Tell the group which person in the story you can best identify with and why.
7. Have each participant respond to the question, Can you recall a time in your life when you were powerless to help someone in great need? Share it with the group.
8. Have everyone present tell of a time in his life when he was in great need and no one could help except Christ.
9. Close the meeting with brief prayers of thanks and dedication.

This format will work in many small group situations. It includes scripture study, personal sharing about relevant concepts, prayer, and deep fellowship. That is what small groups are all about.

CHAPTER ELEVEN

KEEPING THE GROUP ALIVE

Many groups begin with all participants enthusiastic and eager. Then after several weeks the steam goes out of their meetings and no one seems to know why. This may be very natural. Some groups should die and be quietly buried without apology. Others ought to be kept alive for the positive ministry they provide for the participants.

How can you keep a group going? How can you keep alert to the real needs of participants and facilitate honest interaction? How can you help a member be open to the Spirit of God and free to share genuine testimony? Groups grow or die by principles as real as those applying to gravity and electricity. Some of these were listed tongue-in-cheek by Clyde Reid in "Fifteen Ways to Squelch a Small Group":

"1. Dominate the group from the beginning. Establish yourself as the authority on all matters that may come before the group. Make all the basic decisions yourself while giving the impression of a democratic spirit.

"2. Pay no attention to the needs and interests of the members. Most people don't know what is best for them anyhow.

"3. Keep the discussion on a theoretical plane, preferably in the realm of theology and philosophy. Mention names like Kant and Tillich occasionally to make the others feel inferior.

"4. If possible, establish yourself as the teacher of

the group and deliver a learned lecture at each meeting. (This carries a rock-bound guarantee that the group won't last more than three months!)

"5. Don't permit the fiction to arise that group members should take turns leading the discussion. They're liable to get too interested and keep the group alive in spite of your efforts.

"6. Never allow group members to share anything personal. Change the subject to a nice safe intellectual discussion when this happens. That way they won't get too involved with each other at a depth level. Groups in which this happens become devilishly hard to squelch.

"7. By all means, don't encourage all members of the group to express themselves. Limit the participation to the more vocal, intellectual members to keep the conversation on a high plane of sophistication. They will bore each other to sleep.

"8. Don't urge the silent members of the group to speak up. They might get the idea that you really care about them and that their ideas count after all. They will be more difficult to discourage as a result.

"9. Allow one or two persons to dominate the discussion. That way the others will become quietly angry and the group will fold up in no time. By all means, don't point out to the dominators what they are doing. This might lead to some hurt feelings and personal growth—things to be avoided at all costs.

"10. Keep the small group too large for the members to really get to know each other. By all means have at least twenty or twenty-five members in order to do this.

"11. Include a long business meeting with each group session and bore everyone to tears. The group will rapidly wither.

124

"12. Arrange the seats in formal rows like a classroom. Don't permit informality to sneak in by sitting in a friendly circle. In that situation members might feel encouraged to express themselves and not want to give up the group.

"13. Answer all questions yourself. Don't let group members speak to each other or answer each other's questions. What do they know that you can't say better?

"14. By all means don't let group members express any hostility they may feel toward each other. You may find them understanding each other too well as a result, and the group will continue.

"15. Complain at every meeting about how few people have turned out. This will give members a size-consciousness and sense of guilt. They will either quit coming or invite their friends, and the small group will soon grow into oblivion—it will become a large group.

"Note: It is recommended that you, as group leader, express your own unique personality in applying these rules. There is a method that is uniquely yours. (You may have found ways to squelch a group that haven't even been thought of yet.) If you follow any one of these rules with dogged persistence, however, you need not fear. You will have expressed yourself. The group will certainly collapse, for you will have violated a principle of human nature."

—From *Groups Alive—Church Alive*
(Harper and Row)

To keep the meeting alive several principles will need to be observed. Periodic evaluation to keep leaders tuned in to what's really happening—or not happening—in the group is important also.

EVALUATION QUESTIONS

Physical Arrangements
1. Was the group small enough (not over 12) for all to share?
2. Did the members sit in a close circle?
3. Did the meeting start and end on time?
4. Was everyone comfortable (was the lighting adequate, the temperature right)?
5. If refreshments were served, did they enhance the spirit of fellowship—or become the center of attention?
6. Did someone help the host put the furniture back in place after the meeting?

Content Level
1. Was the discussion topic relevant to life?
2. Were scriptures used?
3. Did everyone have scriptures in hand?
4. Did anyone in the group move toward a more affirmative answer to these five basic questions:
   a. Do I really know who Jesus is?
   b. Have I made a genuine commitment to him?
   c. Can I relate this commitment to daily life?
   d. Can I share my experience of Christ with others?
   e. Am I involved in bringing God's kingdom on earth?
5. Was an invitation to the larger corporate church services extended?

Feeling Level
1. Was anyone embarrassed during the meeting?
2. Was the conversation personal or theoretical?

126

3. Did all participate? If not, did all feel free to participate?

Future Improvements
1. Was the meeting evaluated afterwards?
2. Was note made of personal needs requiring a follow-up visit to the home?
3. Is the group growing, standing still, or gradually dying? (This first should be asked after a month or two, and then only periodically.)

The chief reasons why groups die appear to include the following:
1. Leaders and participants do not take the group seriously enough to pray and prepare before the meeting.
2. The leaders are insensitive or inadequate.
3. There are no disciplines or depth in the group.
4. Members are unwilling to be open, honest, and personal in conversation.
5. A clique spirit develops which only feeds members' need for approval.
6. Attention is focused on the "content level" of the meeting, with the vital "feeling or process" level being ignored.
7. The content level is shallow because members refuse to grapple with life's real issues.

The following ways to bring a stale small group back to life were listed in the *Open Circle Newsletter* (Faith at Work):

"1. Take a few moments to let each person tell what has happened to him the week past. Mention events, problems, needs, and answers which seem important to you.

"2. Read a scripture passage and see whether it applies to concrete situations in which members of the group find themselves, and to their current needs and desires.

"3. Spend some time in silence—from one to five minutes as a start. The group leader may suggest several questions to consider during the quiet time. For example: What do you feel is God's next step for you? Is there any relationship in your home, church, or neighborhood that God would have you change? Where is your growing edge? In what direction is God nudging you?

"If it seems helpful, use pencil and paper to jot down thoughts that come to you during meditation.

"4. Go around the circle, giving each person an opportunity to say what thoughts came to him. Do not criticize these statements or comment extensively on them. If someone makes a general statement such as, "I should be more thoughtful," ask him to pin it down to particular situations. Thoughtful to whom? In what areas?

"5. Pray around the circle, using the first person singular and being specific. One week let each person pray for someone else in the group—the person on his left, for example. The next week, let each one pray for himself.

"6. Agree to pray for one another at least once a day, praying not in generalities but for the definite things that have been mentioned.

"7. During the week, make note of those concerns which you want to bring to the next group meeting. Determine to share your joys and triumphs as well as your needs and problems."

128

Sam Shoemaker was reflecting on why groups die when he said:

"There is no way to guarantee the unbroken flow of the Spirit in the Church or in a movement, so there is no way to guarantee the upward progress of the small group. It has been my experience that often a group is like a baby—it may be heavier at birth than soon after when it begins to lose. But care, food, and love are likely to insure the continuation of the baby's life, so there are usually ways to continue the group. There will be some weeks when it is good, some when it is less good, some when it is poor. Rufus Jones once said of a Quaker meeting he attended that it was 'A new high in lows.' We have all been to such meetings. Maybe the group has served its purposes and should break up with its members going on to some other kind of formation. But many a group begins declining from recognizable causes:

1. It has gone 'churchy,' formal, busy, and needs to come back under the simplicity of the Spirit.

2. It has gotten enmeshed in the technicalities of religion itself and forgotten its purpose through interest in its means.

3. There is no overflow into the lives of others outside the group, so it is self-centered and grows stale."

—*With the Holy Spirit with Fire,* Harper, page 113.

A helpful pamphlet, *The Small Group, A Big Answer,* published by *Guideposts* contains the following suggestions:

"There are three main dangers which small groups must guard against: hogging, bogging, and frogging. One person can *hog* the discussion; an individual can *bog* the group down on an irrelevant matter; or the discussion can move from point to point, *leap-frogging* so much that nothing is accomplished. Here are suggestions for these and other concerns.

"1. Only a few people have done all the talking: Say, 'Some of us talked quite a bit tonight; let's give time now for some of those we haven't heard from yet.'

"2. Someone talks in vague abstractions: Ask, 'Can you give us a personal experience to illustrate that point? A specific example will help us understand what you mean.'

"3. Someone goes off on a tangent: Say, 'That's a very interesting point, Joe. Perhaps you and I can talk about it at length after the meeting, but let's get back now to our topic for tonight.'

"4. A problem of group concern the week before is overlooked: Say, 'Last week, Sara, we said we'd pray about your relationship with your mother-in-law. What has happened since?' "

To keep meetings alive a leader will need to be aware of some common problems in small group meetings.

1. *The dominator.* Usually in every group there is someone who dominates the discussion and takes too much time putting forth his views.

2. *Apathy.* Sometimes the discussion becomes sluggish, members show a lack of interest, and people begin glancing at their watches.

3. *The avoidance of depth.* Many groups will shy away from any discussion which is personal or has any depth. Some hide behind abstract theories or deal in superficialities. When a group does not have the strength and courage to discuss openly any of the real problems of life, it is in trouble.

4. *Inadequate physical arrangements.* Sometimes the

circle is too large. Occasionally in a big room people may be hesitant to move the furniture closer. The lighting may be inadequate, or the one in charge may have trouble trying to lead an informal discussion in a formal setting (perhaps at church).

5. *The shy person.* No one should be forced to share in a group discussion; however, the leader can help draw out quiet members by looking at them in such a way that they know they are being encouraged to participate when they feel ready. Occasionally the leader can say, "Anyone who hasn't spoken yet and would like to share will be given an opportunity."

6. *A clash of personalities.* When two people disagree violently the leader can help by having each party state his position and the other person restate it to his satisfaction. Sometimes the leader may get those in disagreement to preface their remarks with something like "In my humble opinion it appears this way. . . ."

7. *Getting started.* The first fifteen minutes in a meeting are the most crucial. In order to establish rapport and get everyone at ease and ready to enter into discussion, the leader must be relaxed and natural, treat all present with respect, and encourage them to participate.

8. *Verbosity.* This is the greatest problem in most groups. The untrained leader tends to panic and in his nervousness dominates the discussion by too much talking. He should say only enough to set the stage, get the discussion rolling, and then speak only when it is necessary to keep things going. He is a "facilitator."

9. *Tangents.* Occasionally someone will throw in something irrevelant and take the group in a direction away from the agreed topic. Some freedom should be allowed, but in cases like this the leader should ask another question in order to bring the group back to the stated topic.

10. *Ego.* The leader may have to sacrifice his own image at times for the welfare of the group. Only a mature person will avoid taking advantage of situations in which he might look bad if he didn't know the answer, or did not know how to control the situation.

11. *Balanced discussion.* A constant flow back and forth between spontaneity and directed discussion is the challenge of the good leader. He should have a destination in mind yet allow the participants great flexibility.

12. *Evaluation.* To assist leaders in evaluating the effectiveness of a meeting, questions are provided on page 126 in this book.

Many problems can arise in a group. All persons have psychological and spiritual needs and drives. In the small group setting these problems continually pop up and should be anticipated.

The major problem of leading small groups is the task of understanding individuals and their needs, knowing what is happening during the meeting, and developing the necessary sensitivity to guide the group so that all benefit. This is a big order for any person. Anyone, however, can become a better group leader with persistent effort, willingness to fail and to learn from that experience.

CHAPTER TWELVE

CROSS-SECTION OF MINISTERIAL OPINION - 1971

Ten years ago the attitude in the Saints Church toward groups was somewhat different than today. Few World Church or local congregational leaders were familiar with or in favor of utilizing this means of ministry. Things have changed. To determine the present climate, a simple survey was mailed in the fall of 1971 to 200 full-time appointee ministers in the United States and Canada. The questionnaire was designed to sample leadership attitudes and current involvement in small group meetings. Those receiving it were key men in the church.

Sixty-five of the 200 responded. These included three apostles, four regional administrators, eighteen district presidents, seven stake presidents, three Presidents of Seventy, two bishops, twenty missionaries, and eight others. Some of the questions and responses follow:

"Are there any small group meetings now being held in your jurisdiction (congregation, stake, or district)?

> Yes—39
>
> No—4
>
> No reply—22

"Are you aware of any small groups held in your jurisdiction in the past three years?

> Yes—42
>
> No—20
>
> No reply—3

*"Are you presently meeting regularly with some
type of small informal group (prayer breakfast, sharing
group, scripture study, etc.)?*

> Yes—22
> No—43

"If not, would you like to?

> Yes—23
> No—1
> No reply—19

*"Do you desire some type of training in your area
for potential leaders of small groups?*

> Yes—45
> No—4
> Maybe—9
> No reply—7

"What value, if any, do you see in small groups?"

A paragraph was allotted for replying to the preceding question. The following are sample comments:

"Small group ministry has transformed one of the congregations in this stake. A year ago the congregation was plagued with apathy, bitterness, marital tensions, etc. Small group meetings were initiated, and in one year the congregation has been reactivated and is now one of the strongest in the stake. Many individuals and several families have been restored to a wholesome church life."—Gene Austin, Sr. (stake president)

"Frances [wife] and I participate in two small groups. One is working on finding trust and true fellowship, and the other is seeking, through experimentation, to find ways to worship that are truly enabling."—C. D. Neff (apostle)

"Small groups offer exciting possibilities. Leadership is the key (i.e. leaders' personality and character qualifications and ability to understand, appreciate, and relate to each person in the group). Many now leading need top drawer training to better qualify. It is the best method I've been able to use in my ministry—including so-called cottage meetings."—Phil Moore (district president)

"Advantages are evangelistic outreach and membership renewal. I would like to see several scripture groups going in our stakes."—Sylvester R. Coleman (stake president)

"Advantages are self-understanding, development of relationships, growth, and renewal."—E. W. Dickens (missionary)

"I feel small groups are an answer to declining church interest. However, you do need trained and skilled personnel to be leaders, and this poses problems."—J. D. Overly (district president)

"Small groups get people acquainted meaningfully and build fellowship based on understanding of ideas and people."—R. V. Webb (regional administrator)

"The greatest value of small groups that I can see is the opportunity to deepen relationships between people."—Loyd Adams (former stake president)

"If this small group program was started, Center Stake would multiply its baptismal record simply because someone cared enough to be personal in a mass media day. Small groups help bring positive trust that is needed to advance the cause of Zion."—Ward E. Francis (stake evangelism worker)

"As Elton Trueblood has said, small groups are a key to church renewal in our time."—Norman Page (district president)

"The modern society of the United States has fragmented the close fellowship which at one time existed among church members. The midweek prayer service for the entire congregation seems to have lost its effectiveness, thus the majority never attend. It seems to me that the small group, if properly directed, will tend to build close fellowship on a sound basis."—Duane H. Birks (district president)

"The small group and lay ministry emphasis suggested by Trueblood may be our last hope."—John W. Bradley (district president)

"Small groups help to reach people. I have found a freedom of expression where no one feels condemned for speaking what he or she thinks. I have in mind particularly a young lady who has become activated toward the church through such small group fellowship."—Ray Ashenhurst (district president)

"Persons feel more free to ask questions, discuss, and be open in their feelings and opinions. They get to know each other and become interested in each other's joys, sorrows, achievements, needs, etc."—Charles V. Graham (former stake president)

"While it is probably the most effective way to bring people to Christ in the present age, it is not a new idea; the early missionaries won many to Christ and the church through small group meetings in the homes of saints and friends. We need a continuing training program for the local ministry in this type of evangelism."—Calvin French (stake president)

"In the hands of the well-trained it is valuable. In the hands of poorly trained, it can be lethal!"—A. H. Yale (director of priesthood education—School of Restoration)

"Small groups have a freedom of expression seldom possible in larger groups."—Don Lents (apostle)

"It appears to me that the greatest value of small groups is in the reawakening of members to the baptism covenant, the opening of opportunities to bring the message to friends, and follow-up after baptism. I have noticed the opportunities

136

are great for uniting 'split families.' "—Eugene Chaney (district president)

"Excellent results in drawing members together and creating a feeling of concern and love for one another."—Merle Harford (district president)

"Involvement of people as persons on person-to-person sharing and caring level. It also motivates people to participate. We have a monthly men's prayer breakfast in Columbus, Ohio."—Roy Leamon (stake bishop)

"Small interaction groups have proven themselves by allowing persons to really understand one another because of the size of the group and the eyeball to eyeball contact. This is not possible in most gatherings typified by our present congregational life-style."—Gary B. Beebe (regional administrator)

"I am 100 percent for small groups."—Cecil R. Ettinger (apostle)

"People can be motivated and trained toward Christian devotion and service better in small groups than in any other way. They also come to share much more richly in Christian fellowship and warmth."—Luther S. Troyer (evangelist)

"Small groups give each a chance to participate. They are nonjudgmental and provide therapeutic catharsis. They also help participants to be genuine and go beyond simple cordial expression into the deeper conversional process."—A. M. Pelletier (district president)

"I have a Master's degree in group administration, and much of my professional time in an educational career is based on group work philosophy and principles. If you are asking about small group evangelism, I really have little background here, but I have much more faith in the principle than in the fifty-minute sermon, series preaching, and mass campaign."—Lee Hart (department executive)

"It is an effective method of attracting and getting people

involved and laying foundations for adjustments in their lives that lead to conversion."—A. F. Gibbs (missionary)

"Small groups stimulate friendships and people become willing to trust one another. They also stimulate people to pray and testify."—William Clinefelter (district president)

Other comments:

"I believe the future of the church is dependent on the deep personal ministries of the Spirit of Christ transmitted by depth relationships possible in small groups."—Dr. Gerald Knutson (Ph.D. in educational psychology, high priest, pastor at Stillwater, Oklahoma, and staff administrator at Oklahoma State University)

"I feel this is one of the best methods for reaching people we have. It is very easy for nonmembers to fit into these groups because there is no pressure. They feel free to express their own viewpoint, and because of this they are free to accept our point of view. Small groups have helped our branch very much."—Jack Basse (high priest, Tulsa Stake missionary)

"When I think of both evangelism and worship I find myself a strong proponent of the small group system, mainly because I see some things that need to be done in the lives of individuals which can't be done in a sanctuary. We need to start where people are. I feel that if we really work in developing this method, it can have all kinds of possibilities. The chief danger is the temptation to institutionalize the small group to the point of rigidity; its genius is spontaneity and fluidity. Small groups may tend to become closed corporations. They may become like some of our congregations, setting their sights supremely upon themselves and using their resources for self-preservation. Leadership must see small groups as powerful units."—Apostle Neff (reported in the *University Bulletin*)

"I am happy to share with you from our experience in small group study. I believe in the approach wholly and fervently. Shortly after the article in *Guidelines* [September 1958] was written, other people became interested and formed a second group. About that time a third group began studying with my brother, Patriarch James A. Thomas. Then we took on a third class ourselves, made up of older adults—many of them parents of our first group. James then began a second group. Under the urging of Presiding Elder Jerry Runkle, the work was expanded, and for a long time a total of nine small groups (each week) were being held in the homes."—Olive Mortimore, Lamoni, Iowa (in a letter to the author)

Sister Mortimore goes on to relate how baptisms, ordinations, "renewed" members, and service to the church and community resulted from the stimulation of these small groups meetings.

A lengthy but excellent response to the survey came from Roy Cheville, presiding patriarch:

"The small face-to-face group meeting is indispensable. Jesus used it with his three men, with his twelve men, with families in homes, and in other situations. Certainly, it is an indispensable part of my own ministry. This week four of us sat around a table for two and a half hours after the evening meal. We talked frankly and searchingly. I had a sense of communion with a father and his two sons, one of them recently married. I could converse as I would not and could not with a large congregation. Nor could I have done this with a pickup small group.

"Recently, too, I invited four men to my apartment for a bachelor's meal. One was a nonmember trying to find his way. The circle after supper was a testimonial fellowship. But I find some persons appear to think that the main thing is that the group be small. These give little attention to bringing together persons who can blend in searching and sharing. Then, too, I find some talking as if this is a newly discovered method that is going to save the church.

"Another thing we shall do well to watch is compliance with some new hobby in coming together. Recently I learned of such a group of young persons. The problem was the leader. The latest thing was to sit on the floor and chew chips and cookies and 'confess.' There are many of these novelty emphases that can sidetrack what we want to accomplish.

"Just now there has been a high point of planning nothing. We just let things come up. This has applied to camps and conferences, and more. We are seeing that it is possible to have purpose and plans and also flexibility. There has been focus on 'rap sessions' and the like, and some of these have not turned out well. The opposite is the 'cottage meeting' in which there is a fixed procedure of slides and scriptures. Neither is to be taken as the only way.

" 'Scripture reading' is currently in the air. Much of this involves reading for emotional warmth and for the specific answering of questions. The latter often involves opening the Bible and pointing to a passage that is supposed to provide an answer to some question.

"We need insight about the ministering of the Holy Spirit. Some strange things happen that are attributed to 'the Spirit.' The small group meeting can have marked stress on 'inspiration' and 'gifts.'

"I write this that we may develop soundness of purpose, plan, and prophecy in our small group meetings. Such meetings need to be interpreted and used in the context of our total program. A person coming into our church should feel the pulse and purpose of both the congregation and the inclusive church. This is not an either-or but a both-and situation. We need to provide small group ministries and congregational fellowship.

140

"Our church needs so much the what, why, how, and who of these. One basic possibility is the functioning of the family as a small group conference. We need some small groups in which persons of different generations come together. We need staff sessions in which persons get together for 'common consent.' We need small groups in which persons of diverse cultures and conceptions come together. One of our foremost needs is small groups in which world church men sit in two-way conversation with members of diverse ages and viewpoints."

The survey questionnaire responses indicate that many small groups are now in progress in the church across the United States and Canada. The attitude of appointee leadership is certainly positive, although less than half of the respondents were actually involved in small groups themselves. Many wrote a note explaining that their travel schedule was a factor in preventing regular participation.

A desire for some systematic training for leaders was strongly indicated. In the question concerning the desire for leadership training, a total of 58 responded as follows: Yes—45; No—4; Maybe—9.

The survey and comments reveal that a very favorable climate exists toward the small group method as a viable form of ministry in the church. Even though there has been no official training program for leaders or local workers as yet, a quickened and timely interest in small groups has developed throughout the church. Very little material has been produced. The expansion into this area of ministry may necessarily continue to go slowly. Leadership training and educational materials hopefully will be forthcoming soon. A deepening of personal ministry and greater outreach in local churches through small group meetings would seem to be a certainty in the days ahead.

CHAPTER THIRTEEN

PILOT PROJECT ON ATTITUDE CHANGE

This chapter is a brief summary of a pilot project conducted on attitude change through small encounter groups at the University of Tulsa in 1969 while I was completing requirements for a graduate degree in guidance and counseling. Under the guidance of Dr. Gaylin Wallace I was permitted to use religious terms for measuring thirty-three subjects' attitudes before and after participation in small encounter group meetings. Since the university was interested only in the method of research, the subject matter to be measured was optional. Wanting to relate the insights of modern education to the church, I selected fifteen religious terms to measure in the experiment. The following were used to measure the subjects evaluative perception before and after the group meetings.

1. Me . . . self
2. Group leader
3. Priesthood
4. Christ
5. God
6. Scriptures
7. Family
8. People in general
9. Serving others
10. Prayer
11. Tithing
12. Enemies
13. Communion
14. Church
15. People in my home church

The purpose of the project was to determine if the effect of the small encounter group meeting produced any significant change in the attitudes of the participants. The problem investigated was stated specifically, "Would perception which people hold before small encounter group experiences change significantly after experiencing the encounter group?" It was thought that the dynamic interactions between individuals in the encounter group would make it almost impossible for them not to be influenced to some degree. The question concerned the degree of change, if the change would be positive or negative, and if it would be really significant.

The focus was on measuring the evaluative perceptions of the individuals involved in these small group meetings. Evaluative perception is one of the major components of attitude. Change in this area would reveal some alterations in the subject's basic attitudes. If attitudes form a prime basis for behavior, as many educators contend, this could be related to the church's approach to helping people change.

Arrangements were made for thirty-three subjects in three separate encounter groups to be held on three different weekends. These were marathon meetings consisting of several uninterrupted hours spreading over a two-day period. (They were not the "sensitivity type.") A semantic differential attitude measuring device (Osgood and Tannenbaum) was designed for the project, using twenty bipolar adjectives to measure the evaluative perception of the subjects on the fifteen religious concepts. The semantic differential has been proved a reliable scientific instrument for measuring attitudes. In repeated tests the margin of error has been well below the accepted level. (A sample is included at the end of this chapter.)

The groups in the project were designated as A, B, and C. Group A had thirteen subjects, group B, twelve, and group C, eight. Group A was comprised of men and women between the ages of twenty-five and fifty. All but two had previously been together for six weekly class sessions at the Tulsa

144

Central Church. I had taught them in a class called "Communication with Your Companion." Ten of the thirteen were married couples.

Group A was led by a professional encounter group leader, Marian Ferguson, from the Psychological Testing Department of the Tulsa Public School System.

Participants in Group A met at the Western Hills State Lodge at Wagoner, Oklahoma, from 7:00 p.m. Friday to 4:00 p.m. Saturday for a total of fifteen hours, interrupted only by four hours of sleep. The pretest was given to each subject immediately upon arrival at the lodge. The post-test was given just before departure for home.

Group B was comprised of twelve subjects ages twenty-one to fifty. All were ordained ministers from the Skiatook, Oklahoma, congregation. This group met at the church recreation building in Sperry, Oklahoma, on a Sunday from 7:00 a.m. to 5:00 p.m. for a total of ten continuous hours. No meals were served during this period (except for fruit juices and coffee) thus permitting maximum time for interaction. I served as leader of this group. As in Group A the pretest was given to all members upon their arrival and the post-test given at the conclusion.

Group C was comprised of eight young adults, ages twenty-two to forty. Two were married, two were divorced, and the other four were young adults. They met at the Western Hills State Lodge at Wagoner, Oklahoma, from 8:00 p.m. Friday to 1:00 p.m. Saturday for a total of seventeen continuous hours. They met continuously without sleep (except for several participants who napped briefly). I was the leader of this group also.

The semantic differential measuring instrument prepared for this study was administered to each person before and after the encounter group experience. The testing procedure was explained to all participants before the actual experience of interacting began. The instruments were given out, with pencils, and the brief instructions at the top of the paper read aloud. Questions were allowed so everyone would understand the procedure. All were asked to work quickly, checking their general first impression. Slips of paper with marked numbers were drawn by each subject as an identifying code number to mark at the top of the instrument in order to protect the subject's anonymity and to match pretest with post-test.

These meetings proceeded on a rather unstructured basis. The leader sought only to facilitate honest interaction between the participants. No particular input of information was offered. The present feelings of the subjects was the material dealt with as the group members sought to relate to each other and communicate genuinely. No communication games were played. No unusual techniques were employed. Participants were simply sharing as honestly and genuinely as possible.

There were times of uneasiness but no outburst of anger or obvious aggression. There was no confession of deep secrets or unusual personal revelations. Great respect was shown to each person, and all who participated reported a general feeling of well-being afterwards. Some did share personal hopes or fears for the future. At times there were long silences. The greatest single characteristic of the groups was a feeling of acceptance by the others. As the groups progressed the trust-level between participants increased and honest sharing of inner feelings deepened. As participants felt accepted by the group they appeared to experience greater self-acceptance and inner peace. The measurements before and afterward indicated that they felt a more positive perception of people in general and the world around them.

Because this was conducted as a research pilot project for the university no discussions of a religious nature were introduced except as they came up naturally in relation to hopes, fears, and life purposes. Though tiring, all three small group meetings were pleasant experiences, and those who participated indicated their willingness to do so again if they were needed.

Following the three weekend marathon meetings, scores from the pretest and post-test semantic differential attitude measuring instrument were fed into the university computer. A statistical analysis of the results was made. Scores are listed at the end of this chapter. (The statistical formula used to determine the significance of change of attitude was the "T" statistic.)

I quote from the evaluation statement: "From the data it seems reasonable to conclude that the interaction of the small basic encounter group does produce change in the attitudes of individuals. The small group appears to be a valid method of behavior change which holds many possibilities for persons in our society responsible for molding attitudes and modifying behavior."

The religious terms used for the measurement of attitude change for this project indicate that churches might employ some form of small groups in their overall programs of influencing persons. The results of a more positive feeling toward God and those concepts associated with religion in these three groups hold significant implication for concerned church leaders.

Since the terms used in the measurement were not discussed as topics yet there was a positive change toward them, it would appear that the small group can assist an individual in his total perceptions in life. In order to produce changed attitudes there does not always have to be a particular informational input into the groups. While information remains very important, the experience of increased trust toward others in the group, increased self-awareness, and the tendency toward openness may all be factors which foster greater positive change in attitudes toward concepts which deal with the relationships in life. The curriculum in these groups was simply the lives of the participants, their backgrounds, experiences, and general character. Naturally this approach is not recommended for most other small groups.

The results of this study agree with the claims of Alcoholics Anonymous, Synanon (for drug addicts), and other self-help organizations which rely heavily upon the dynamics of the small group meeting where participants are interacting in honesty and openness and holding each other accountable. Dynamic interaction in a small group of accepting persons can facilitate growth and positive change.

In Group A a significant change (using the "T" statistic) occurred in a total of five of the fifteen concepts measured. In Group B a significant change occurred in nine of the concepts. In Group C a significant change occurred in three concepts. While the people in Group C seemed to have the most fun being together (nearer the same age and background) they reported the least amount of significant change in attitude. Attitude change is not dependent on pleasant experience. In fact, those experiences which ultimately prove to be of most worth in terms of emotional growth and maturity may be the least enjoyable. Scripture supports the idea that persons wanting to grow in emotional maturity may have to be willing to suffer.

Group B reported the most change in number of concepts which were considered statistically significant in altered attitudes. These ministers came together with the greatest commitment to a serious purpose in their gathering. This may have contributed to the results. They had the least comfortable surroundings for their group, meeting in a church basement, and they fasted during the ten-hour period.
148

It should be added that there were many unknown variables operating in each group to account for some of the differences in the amount of change. Other factors need more testing, such as the lasting effect of the change, comparing length of meetings to change, male and female attitudes, and background. A significant conclusion of the experimental project is that positive attitude change does not always depend on information. It can occur in the warm interpersonal relationships which develop in small groups where intimacy and primary contacts are possible.

Leaders in society responsible for helping to bring about positive change in behavior will find the small group process a helpful technique. As world population increases and impersonal attitudes become more prevalent the small group may become more necessary for personality development and attitude change. The church cannot ignore this method and its tremendous possibilities.

The current interest of leaders in industry, education, and religious organizations in small groups seems to be justified from the indications of this study. While only a few of the total concepts measured were changed significantly the fact that any significant change occurred is reason for hope and further investigation into the dynamics of the small group method. This project tested (tentatively) only one type of small group. There are many types and methods employed by persons interested in small groups. This project agrees with the convictions held by many social scientists. Much research and exploration need to be done to identify factors involved in changing human behavior. More investigation in ways to assist persons toward growth and maturity is open for study. Whatever the future uncovers, it is apparent that the small group will be utilized, in some form, in an increasing degree.

SEMANTIC DIFFERENTIAL—Attitude Test

(SAMPLE TEST FORM)   1. Male_____   4. After_________

2. Female__   5. Code No._____

Concept to Rate: <u>FRIENDS</u>   3. Before________

Mark with an "X" or checkmark the spot between the two adjectives which best represents your immediate feelings concerning the concept above. Work rather quickly recording your general first impression. Some of the words may not seem to fit, but that is all right. Mark something on each line. The middle spot is a neutral mark.

1. Good	__ __ __ __ __ __ __ __	Bad
2. Unfair	__ __ __ __ __ __ __ __	Fair
3. Sincere	__ __ __ __ __ __ __ __	Insincere
4. Cruel	__ __ __ __ __ __ __ __	Kind
5. Dull	__ __ __ __ __ __ __ __	Interesting
6. Slow	__ __ __ __ __ __ __ __	Fast
7. Superior	__ __ __ __ __ __ __ __	Inferior
8. Pleasant	__ __ __ __ __ __ __ __	Unpleasant
9. Incompetent	__ __ __ __ __ __ __ __	Competent
10. Accepting	__ __ __ __ __ __ __ __	Critical
11. Pleasing	__ __ __ __ __ __ __ __	Annoying
12. Procastina-ting	__ __ __ __ __ __ __ __	Punctual
13. Handsome	__ __ __ __ __ __ __ __	Ugly
14. Messy	__ __ __ __ __ __ __ __	Neat
15. Relaxed	__ __ __ __ __ __ __ __	Tense
16. Argumenta-tive	__ __ __ __ __ __ __ __	Peaceful
17. Quiet	__ __ __ __ __ __ __ __	Loud
18. Undependable	__ __ __ __ __ __ __ __	Dependable
19. Feminine	__ __ __ __ __ __ __ __	Masculine
20. Untrust-worthy	__ __ __ __ __ __ __ __	Trustworthy

TABLE ONE

PRETEST AND POST-TEST COMPARISON
OF MEAN SCORE DIFFERENCES
FOR GROUP A (thirteen subjects—met nineteen hours)

CONCEPTS	MEAN SCORES			"T" test
	Post-test	Pretest	N	Statistic
1. Me . . . self	103	101	13	.93
2. Group leader	110	111	11	.12
* 3. Ministers	103	96	13	2.37
4. Christ	132	129	2	2.33
5. God	122	118	12	1.58
6. Scriptures	103	95	12	1.52
* 7. Family	113	105	12	3.84
8. People in general	98	96	12	.74
9. Serving others	106	105	11	.31
10. Prayer	105	102	11	1.47
*11. Tithing	97	93	12	3.55
12. Enemies	65	70	12	1.21
*13. Communion	105	101	12	1.91
*14. Church	102	98	12	2.16
15. People in home church	101	96	12	1.46
Average	103	99		

*Mean *post-test* response differs significantly from mean *pretest* response, indicating attitude change was altered significantly as a result of the small group meeting.

TABLE TWO

PRETEST AND POST-TEST COMPARISON
OF MEAN SCORE DIFFERENCES
FOR Group B

(twelve subjects all priesthood, met for ten hours)

CONCEPTS	MEAN SCORE		N	"T" test
	Post-test	Pretest		Statistics
* 1. Me . . . self	106	100	10	1.84
* 2. Group leader	124	117	10	1.90
* 3. Ministers	120	108	10	2.32
4. Christ	134	131	10	.69
5. God	132	130	10	1.01
* 6. Scriptures	118	109	10	2.60
* 7. Family	114	105	9	3.25
8. People in general	103	100	10	1.69
* 9. Serving others	107	101	10	1.90
*10. Prayer	117	107	11	2.11
11. Tithing	111	109	10	.77
12. Enemies	75	65	10	1.75
*13. Communion	117	109	10	2.80
14. Church	117	112	10	1.52
*15. People in home church	113	104	10	2.96
Average	111	102		

*Mean *post-test* response differs significantly from mean *pretest* response, indicating attitude change was altered significantly as a result of the small group meeting.

TABLE THREE

PRETEST AND POST-TEST COMPARISON OF MEAN SCORE DIFFERENCES

FOR GROUP C (eight subjects, met for seventeen hours)

CONCEPT	MEAN SCORE			N		"T" test statistic
	Post-test	Pretest				
* 1. Me . . . self	112	94		7		2.84
2. Group leader	122	113		7		1.85
3. Ministers	110	101		7		1.42
* 4. Christ	134	126		7		2.39
5. God	131	125		6		.78
6. Scriptures	106	98		7		1.43
7. Family	107	103		7		.79
8. People in general	99	94		7		1.26
9. Serving others	107	101		7		1.65
10. Prayer	116	109		7		1.24
11. Tithing	106	99		7		1.43
*12. Enemies	82	66		7		2.44
13. Communion	115	106		7		1.92
14. Church	107	102		7		.83
15. People in home church	104	98		7		1.59
Average	111	102				

*Mean *post-test* response differs significantly from mean *pretest* response, indicating attitude change was altered significantly as a result of the small group meeting.

GRAPHIC REPRESENTATION*
OF MEAN-SCALE VALUES BEFORE AND AFTER ENCOUNTER GROUP

CONCEPT (Summary of all fifteen)

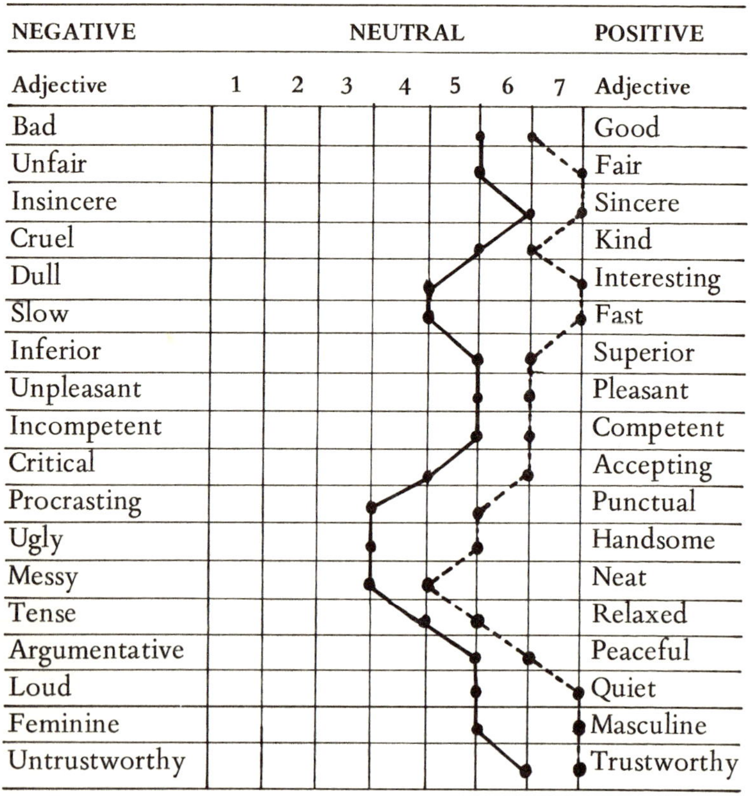

NEGATIVE		NEUTRAL						POSITIVE
Adjective	1	2	3	4	5	6	7	Adjective
Bad								Good
Unfair								Fair
Insincere								Sincere
Cruel								Kind
Dull								Interesting
Slow								Fast
Inferior								Superior
Unpleasant								Pleasant
Incompetent								Competent
Critical								Accepting
Procrasting								Punctual
Ugly								Handsome
Messy								Neat
Tense								Relaxed
Argumentative								Peaceful
Loud								Quiet
Feminine								Masculine
Untrustworthy								Trustworthy

———Before Small Group Experience
– – – After Small Group Experience
*Semantic Differential Measuring Instrument

CHAPTER FOURTEEN

SMALL GROUPS IN THE FUTURE

As the church moves ahead it must continue to be responsive to the needs of people, always seeking creative ways to minister. The world will be changing even faster in the future, demanding greater flexibility and creativity on the part of leaders. Toffler uses the term "future shock" to describe the emotional reaction of men in a whirlwind society. Carl Rogers suggests that one of the most serious problems of the century is how much change the human mind can endure before disintegration takes place. The days ahead will demand the best in the church to meet this challenge.

In this fast changing world men will need more than ever "a place to stand." Small groups of loving, accepting, caring people in local congregations will be a vital part of the "ark" to save men from the flood of hate, violence, and disintegration. The church must prepare now to provide this ministry in the future. It must be in the front providing emotional stability and spiritual maturity for persons needing to relate meaningfully to each other in small companies. Former presidential adviser Daniel P. Moynihan says the United States is showing the characteristics now of an individual going through a nervous breakdown. In the quicksand of contemporary change, a solid place to stand will be sought by an increasing number of people. Small groups within the church can provide a haven of emotional rest for weary seekers as well as a door into the redemptive fellowship of Jesus Christ.

Witnessing in the future will be more easily accomplished

in the small group "home-type" meeting. Friends of the church, as well as members who have become inactive, will more readily accept an invitation to an informal session in the nonthreatening atmosphere of a home than to a formal meeting in the sanctuary. The church of the future will have to go where people are if it is to relate to them and share the healing power of the gospel. Small groups will increasingly fill a need in this outreach. The large meeting in the church will not diminish in significance, but the initial contact with nonmembers will become increasingly frequent in homes. Following conversion new Saints need the larger fellowship and corporate worship along with continued small group experiences.

Presiding Patriarch R. A. Cheville says:

"One of the most fruitful expressions in evangelism is bringing into a small group a host of evangelistic persons who will be benefited by the good health of the group. Those adopted may be members or nonmembers. The text and hope of the gospel is shared through being interviewed by persons who radiate good news and good spirit.

"Today, and the more tomorrow, our evangelism will proceed through adopting into spiritually healthful groups friends who are needing the life and the light that can be taught in small circles, in spiritual vision and verve."—*Spiritual Health,* Herald House, page 409.

Dr. Cheville suggests areas for small groups to explore.

"A group has to be doing and thinking significantly if it is to be spiritually healthy—and there are many fields for group exploration. Here are some major ones that are now pressing among the church of Jesus Christ for sound insight and expression:

1. The nature of man as God intended him to be.

156

2. The ministry of the Holy Spirit as God has designed this spirit to function.

3. The church in organizational administration as God expects the church in world mission.

4. The society (Zion) of all mankind as God created men to be, to live together.

5. The gospel of Jesus Christ as God anticipates this good message to function in transforming men's lives.

6. The family as God sees this primary group carrying on in our complex society.

7. The Restoration movement as God plans it to be functioning for the spiritual restoration of persons and society in the living now.

8. The Book of Mormon as God expects it to witness of the Christ in ancient America for today.

"Each great field can be broken down so it can be handled. Thus each group must study and diagnose the church of this very year. We need to survey our programs in personal and spiritual power in light of the mission to be accomplished. The field is unlimited. The need is urgent. Small groups that see this will leave behind the trivia of our conventional society and begin growing with God."—*Ibid.,* pages 409-410.

Clyde Reid shares his vision of the future this way:

"I should like to share a vision and a hope. I have a vision of churches renewed and revitalized, more alive to the present, more involved in the real needs of the people. I see churches in which people are not ashamed to know each other, nor to love each other, nor to share each other's burdens. I see churches in which there is a deeper inner life through a variety of small groups: and because of that vital inner life, a genuine reaching out to the world—a journey inward, journey outward.

"These are groups in which persons find themselves accepted fully and loved for who they are, with all their shortcomings. These are groups which inspire and encourage and support us in our personal crises so that we do not bear them by ourselves and sit lonely in our pews on Sunday morning crying silently inside. These are groups which speak to our deepest needs to be reconciled to our wives and husbands, to communicate with our youth, to know our God, and to triumph over life. This is the deeper meaning of the ministry of pastoral care and the involvement of the laity in that ministry.

"This is not just a utopian vision. I have hopes of this, because I have seen the signs of it alive here and there. It will mean the constant retraining of our leadership—our whole leadership, lay and clergy. It will be a mammoth task but then the Christian church has faced mammoth tasks before."—*Groups Alive—Church Alive*, Harper and Row, pages 30-31.

The necessity for the church to develop congregations with effective, sensitive leaders who are skilled in the small group method will become increasingly evident in the future. Hopeful signs are appearing in many places. Local leaders are responding and searching for information and assistance both in and out of the church. Hopefully this book will be only one of many helps forthcoming for people in the church who want to prepare for more effective service through small group ministry.

Supplementary Material

SMALL GROUP PREPARATION
FOR A PREACHING SERIES

I. Care enough to fast and pray for guidance before and during the meeting. Conduct the meeting as led by the Spirit.

II. Help everyone relax, feel welcome, and at ease.

III. Assist all in attendance to become well acquainted at the very first:
   A. Seat in a close circle (arrange chairs ahead of time).
   B. At the first meeting, serve simple refreshments to guests as they arrive (to encourage conversation and help all to relax).
   C. Go around the circle and share
      1. Name
      2. Place of birth
      3. Some personal information (not vocation or title) such as a nickname

IV. Explain the purpose of the meetings.
   A. To prepare for series coming soon (give dates, etc.)
   B. To get better acquainted (goals in life, problems, things not normally discussed in shallow conversations)
   C. To discuss scripture together and gain new insights

D. To learn to be honest and real with people
E. To pray together for self, church, friends, and series
F. To provide for involvement of all interested in helping the series to build Christ's kingdom (mention committees and work opportunities for all interested in helping)

V. Ask the group to propose two questions on the sermon topics to be presented by the series speaker.

VI. Discuss the particular sermon topic the members like best from the list provided. Have them choose which one to take first, second, etc.

VII. Keep conversation as personal as possible. Avoid a mere "intellectual" discussion. (Try to get the members to speak from their own feelings and not just quote the experts' opinions.) Be a "model" of openness and honesty for the group.

VIII. Close the meeting with prayer of various types on different nights (perhaps standing in a circle . . . but always as led).
A. Ask for names of specific persons to pray for.
B. Ask members to mention personal needs they wish the group to remember that night (and daily) until the next meeting.
C. Pray for the series, the group, the church.
D. Types of prayer:
1. Silent with leader giving amen
2. Lord's Prayer in unison
3. Conversational prayer
4. Volunteers for brief prayer
5. Prearranged prayer by individual for all

IX. Evaluate the meeting afterward with one or two participants. Look for ways to improve next time.

TEN KICK-OFF QUESTIONS FOR SMALL GROUPS

1. What is the most significant thing that has happened to you in the last three years?
2. Where would you live if you could? What would you do there, if money were no object?
3. What kind of person are you (e.g. argumentative, passive)? What would you like to be?
4. What three headlines would you like to see in the newspaper this week? How could you be involved in bringing them to pass?
5. Who is the most important person in your life? Why?
6. If you could have ten minutes with Jesus, what two things would you ask of him?
7. If you could have one thing revealed to you, what would you want it to be?
8. Tell five good things about yourself.
9. Who has helped you the most to grow? How did he (she) do it?
10. What suffering have you known, and what benefit has it brought you?

—Ken Brock (from Faith at Work, March 1968)

MORE GROUP QUESTIONS – TO OPEN MEETINGS

1. What one thing in your life would you like to change?
2. Do you have an individual interest that you sometimes like to pursue by yourself? What?

3. If you failed to do what your friends want, would you feel left out?
4. What one thing most represents you as a person?
5. If you were going to a masquerade party, what animal would you dress like?
6. What do you think love is?
7. What one thing could you honestly thank God for?
8. Do you feel pressure from society on you as a person? How?
9. How do you maintain your individuality? Integrity?
10. What does the word "relevant" mean to you?
11. How do you feel about the expression "inner emptiness"? Have you ever experienced it?
12. What makes you want to escape into solitude? To lose yourself in a crowd?
13. When have you most benfitted from being alone? From fellowship?
14. Where did you attend school in the fifth grade?
15. Name one good remembrance about your father.
16 When was the first time you ever thought about God?
17. What one thing do you fear most?
18. How would you define the ideal friend?
19. Use one word to describe each person in the group.
20. Tell something about a person you admire.
21. What is the biggest problem you have with Christianity?
22. Do you feel really loved by anyone other than your spouse?
23. Describe what you think is the most boring thing about church.
24. What has been the most significant event in your encounter with God or religion?
25. Describe a time when you were angry; what did you say? What do you think caused your anger? How was the feeling expressed (words, deeds)?

26. Being as honest as you can, list basics that shape your life.
27. If you had the power, what one thing would you do to change society?

Small groups can assist the church to "enlarge the circle of fellowship" by developing congregations that have the following (I have borrowed phrases from *Faith at Work*):

A New Goal	*Relationships*	*Not Religion*
	. . . to God in Christ	
	. . . to self	
	. . . to significant others	
	. . . to world	
A New Strategy	*People*	*Not Programs*
	. . . seeing individuals	
	. . . caring—loving	
	. . . being sensitive to human needs	
	. . . feeling the worth of souls	
A New Style	*Vulnerability*	*Not Defensiveness*
	. . . open to each other	
	. . . honest with self and others	
	. . . humble transparency	
	. . . personal commitment to others' needs	
A New Stance	*Involvement*	*Not Pronouncements*
	. . . sacrificing in response to needs	
	. . . identifying with people and situations	
	. . . tackling evils in communities	
	. . . living under the discipline of church fellowship	
A New Vision	*The Future*	*Not the Past*
	. . . respect for the past but focus on future	
	. . . see Zion in process	
	. . . hope and work for the better world emerging	

LAY FELLOWSHIPS
WITH INTEREST IN SMALL GROUPS

INSTITUTE OF CHURCH RENEWAL, 1610 La Vista Road, N.E., Atlanta, Georgia, 30329. Instrumental in the development of the Lay Witness Mission program, the institute supplies groups with study resources, as well as literature and tapes on the "why" and "how" of groups. Ben C. Johnson, the director, has been in consultation with the Presidents of Seventy on several occasions. Materials from the Institute have been augmented for Witnessing Weekends.

INTERNATIONAL CHRISTIAN LEADERSHIP, 1028 Connecticut Ave., N.W., Suite 614, Washington, D.C. 20036 (296-5830). The popular Presidential Prayer Breakfast is sponsored by this group, which exists for the purpose of initiating small breakfast and luncheon groups for government leaders and men in various vocations.

FAITH AT WORK, INC., Suite 210, 100 Century Plaza, Columbia, Maryland 21043. Author Bruce Larson, a Presbyterian minister, is the executive director. This fellowship revolves around a magazine, *Faith at Work*, and a series of area conferences which meet across the nation. Several handbooks on small groups have been published.

THE PITTSBURGH EXPERIMENT, Bengdum Trees Building, Pittsburgh, Pa. 15222. Founded by Dr. Samuel Shoemaker, the "experiment" consists of small groups of men who meet for lunch throughout the city. *Employment Anonymous*, a ministry to unemployed men in the city, is one expression of outreach. The experiment also conducts a radio broadcast, "Faith at Work," over station KOKA. Paul Everett, a Presbyterian minister, serves as executive director.

164

YOKEFELLOWS, 920 Earlham Drive, Richmond, Ind. Founded by Dr. Elton Trueblood, the Yokefellowship consists of people who have banded together in small groups under certain voluntary disciplines. They maintain retreat facilities and promote small groups. The California Yokefellows (209 Park Road, Burlingame, Calif.) have developed a program for small groups using psychological testing called "prayer therapy." William Parker's book *Prayer Can Change Your Life* describes the program.

GUIDEPOSTS MAGAZINE, Carmel, New York, 10512. A group of people in and around *Guideposts* magazine have an interest in promoting the formation of groups. Their pamphlet, *The Small Group, A Big Answer,* is available on request.

AUDIO-VISUAL RESOURCES

CONVERSION PLUS (Tidings). Color or b/w film, 40 min. 16mm. Rental $11.00 in color or $7.00 in b/w. Shows how evangelism happens in small group. Order from TRAV, 341 Ponce De Leon Ave. N.E., Atlanta, Ga. 30308.

CHRISTIAN WITNESS (Cathedral). Set of six color/sound filmstrips, three records, study textbook. $4 kit, $1 each. Number 4 in series, *Room Full of Miracles,* shows potential of small group fellowship in evangelism. Order from TRAV, 341 Ponce De Leon Ave. N.E., Atlanta, Ga. 30308.

GROWTH THROUGH SMALL GROUPS (Yokefellow Institute). Two tapes with study manual, $12.00. In four sides, twenty-two minutes each, Dr. Sam Emerick, director of Yokefellow Institute, presents need for groups, group development, group vitality, and instructions for convener of group seminar. Order from the Yokefellow Institute, 920 Earlham Dr., Richmond, Indiana.

THE CHURCH AND SMALL GROUPS. One tape of two programmed lessons for classes studying for leadership of groups (also workbooks for participants). Prepared by the Presbyterian Church, tapes and workbooks are available from Institute of Church Renewal, 1610 La Vista Rd. N.E., Atlanta, Ga. 30329. Sale $5.50.

TAPE-O-GRAM (Lay Renewal Publications). A monthly tape resource for small groups, $30.00 per year. One side presents topic for discussion and sharing. The other side gives guidance for group life. Order from Lay Renewal Publications, 1610 La Vista Rd., N. E., Atlanta, Georgia 30329.

SMALL GROUP MINISTRY. A cassette tape explaining how ministry can be given through small groups in the congregation. Both theory and practical suggestions are offered. Order from Presidents of Seventy, the Auditorium, 1001 W. Walnut, Independence, Missouri 64051.

An invitational folder containing this information is available in quantities from the Presidents of Seventy Office, the Auditorium, Independence, Missouri.

WHAT IS A SMALL GROUP?

THE SMALL GROUP MEETING IS ONE OF THE FASTEST GROWING METHODS OF CHRISTIAN EDUCATION IN TODAY'S RAPIDLY CHANGING WORLD.

1. **WHAT** is a small group meeting?

   A small group meeting is a relaxed, friendly, discussion by a few people on a topic relating to life and common concerns. Usually meetings last an hour and a half. The sessions are difficult to describe because we have nothing with which to compare in recent experience. A meeting may have four basic ingredients: (1) fun—there is laughter and good fellowship over refreshments, (2) learning—the scriptures are used as a basis of study, (3) worship—the sessions close with prayer of various types, and (4) group sharing—group members try to be honest with each other and move toward self-discovery and reality. Bible study, frank discussion, prayer, and good fellowship are all involved in a good meeting. Often meetings are tremendous but sometimes they are dull, since the sessions are largely unstructured and their success depends on all participants.

2. **WHY** are these meetings being held?

   People today have difficulty finding a place to talk about the real concerns of their heart without ridicule, being judged, or being misunderstood. These meetings are to assist in depth-communication between persons who want to better understand themselves, get to know others more personally, and expand their understanding about

167

God and His purpose in man. The meetings are aimed at growth in love and understanding. A greater emphasis is placed on "feelings" than on knowledge and facts.

3. **WHO is sponsoring this session of small group meetings?** The Reorganized Church of Jesus Christ of Latter Day Saints is the sponsor for all interested persons of any faith. Meetings are usually more successful when a group has members of several different churches represented. Persons with no faith are welcome. No mention is made of who belongs to what church. The search is for mutual help in life.

YOU ARE CORDIALLY INVITED TO SHARE IN A SMALL GROUP DISCUSSION WITH A FEW OF US AT HOME OF:

____

at: ____

on: ____

time: ____

We expect to have a good time and learn considerable as we seek together for deeper understanding. We need your opinions and ideas to share with the others. Please join with us on the above date, if possible, or later when the group decides where and when to meet regularly.

Your Friend,

signed: _______________________________

address: ______________________________

date signed: __________________________

R.S.V.P.

168

SAMPLE

DISCUSSION AND SERMON TOPICS

Theme: *ANCIENT AMERICAN SCRIPTURES WITNESS*
FOR CHRIST

I. *Current Confusion Concerning Christ*

    1. Matt. 1:18-23

    2. I John 5:1-5, 12, 20-21

    3. II John 1:6-11

    4. I Nephi 3:165-175, 183-186

    5. Mosiah 1:102-108

Questions

1. Do you feel there is a growing confusion about the divinity of Christ today (Resurrection and virgin birth, etc.)?

2. What do you think might be some causes of this?

3. Does it really matter what one thinks?

4. Does the virgin birth issue seem important?

5. What has helped you most to develop your faith in Jesus Christ up to this point in your life?

6. What things tend to cause you to forget Jesus in your daily life?

7. How can the Book of Mormon help people have more understanding and faith in Christ?

II. *God Responds to Every Age*

    1. Rev. 22:18-19
      (Deut. 4:2)

    2. Isaiah 29:1-4, 11-18
      (I.V. 11-22)

    3. Ezek. 37:15-19

1. If men were discovered on another planet, could they have a book of scriptures as divine as the Bible?

2. How would one check it out to see if it is true?

3. What is revelation to you?

169

4. Rev. 14:6

5. II Nephi 12:45-66

4. Does God know the needs of every age?

5. Does God seek to help men in every dispensation?

6. Do you believe in angels today?

7. How did the coming of the Book of Mormon meet a need in the present age?

III. *Christ Is the Universal Savior*

1. John 10:9-11, 16

2. III Nephi 5:3-17

3. III Nephi 10:19-26

4. Mosiah 8:31-35

5. II Nephi 6:44-49

1. Does Christ meet universal human needs?

2. What are some basic needs of man's inner life which Christ alone can supply?

3. Do you think Christ knew about the people in Central America while he was in Palestine?

4. Do you believe God sent his Son to this continent after his ministry in Palestine? Why?

5. Can you understand the difficulty of a person's accepting the idea of another book of scripture if he has been taught only the Bible all his life?

6. How does the Ancient American scripture illustrate the fact that God cares for all races and nations equally?

7. How can you share the good news of Christ's ministry recorded in the Book of Mormon with more people?

170

IV. *American Scriptures Witness for Christ*

1. I John 4:2, 14-15

2. Ether 1:77-81

3. Alma 8:93-96

4. Mosiah 8:28-32

5. Mosiah 1:97-102

1. Can anything be bad that points men to believe in Jesus Christ?

2. What does I John 4:2 mean: "Hereby know ye the spirit of God: Every spirit that confesseth that Jesus is come in the flesh is of God"?

3. How does the Book of Mormon witness for Christ?

4. Do you know anyone who has been helped to a faith in Christ by the Book of Mormon?

5. Can you be a Christian and not believe in the Book of Mormon?

6. Has the Book of Mormon helped you understand Christ?

7. How can the Book of Mormon be used today by the church to help more persons come to a deep faith in Jesus Christ?

V. *Christ Teaches Repentance in Book of Mormon*

1. Heb. 6:1-2

2. I John 1:7-10

3. Mosiah 11:101

4. III Nephi 12:28-33

5. III Nephi 4:44-45, 50-52

1. What does repentance mean to you?

2. Can you recall a time when you had to repent?

3. Is the principle of repentance universal and vital?

4. What did Jesus say about repentance in the Book of Mormon?

5. How can the Book of Mormon help to bring modern men to an awareness of the need for repentance?

6. Is repentance in the Book of Mormon and Bible the same?

7. Did Jesus ever repent? Can you be saved without it?

VI. *Christ Teaches Baptism in Book of Mormon*

1. Mark 16:15-17

1. What did your baptism mean to you then? Now? Can you recall the date?

2. Rom. 6:3-5

2. Is baptism an event, principle, or both?

3. II Nephi 13:7-16

3. Is baptism essential for salvation? Why?

4. III Nephi 5:21-28, 34-35

4. What method of baptism did Jesus teach in the Book of Mormon?

5. Moroni 6:1-5

5. Is baptism in the Book of Mormon and Bible the same?

6. Explain your understanding of baptisms—water and spirit.

7. Is the Book of Mormon helpful in clearing up the confusing issue of baptism today? How?

VII. *Promises for America's Future*

1. II Chr. 7:14

1. Is God interested in lands as well as people?

2. Micah 4:1-2

2. Do you feel that God directs history?

3. II Nephi 1:6-23

3. What do you think is ahead for this country?

4. Ether 1:29-35

4. What promise does the Book of Mormon hold for America?

5. Ether 6:1-10

5. What important conditions are necessary for this land to be protected and blessed?

172

6. How can you help your country realize these blessings?

7. Can one person "make a difference" as President Kennedy stated? How can one begin to try to make an impact in today's world?

VIII. *Book of Mormon Fosters Faith*

1. Heb. 6:1-2, 11:6

1. What does faith mean to you?

2. John 6:28

2. What has helped you to have faith in God over the years? What seems to hinder these days?

3. Ether 5:6-13

3. Can you know God or Christ without faith?

4. Moroni 7: 35-44

4. How would the Book of Mormon help anyone to a greater faith in God?

5. Alma 16:143-144, 151-162

5. What does the Book of Mormon say about the importance of faith?

Theme: *CHRIST IN THE BOOK OF MORMON*
(Bible ref. K.J. and I.V. same except as indicated)

Topics

I. Power of Life in Jesus Christ

(Rom. 1:16; Mosiah 3:9, 21; Jacob 3:8-13; II Nephi 12:30-35, 39; II Nephi 13:16-17)

1. Have you been aware of any new power in your life since you started seriously following Christ (to love more, live better, feel a purpose, etc.)?
2. Do you feel the world needs this power today?
3. How do you suppose Christ helps men to love? (overcome habits, etc.)?
4. Which Book of Mormon scriptures do you like best in this selection?

II. Jesus Christ in the Book of Mormon
   (John 10:16; II Nephi 11:39, 43-48; Ether 1:77-78; Helaman 5:66-67; III Nephi 4:44-45, 48, 50-52; Moroni 10:29)
   1. Do you feel there is confusion in the world concerning Christ?
   2. Does it matter to you if Christ was divine or not?
   3. What difference does it make?
   4. How does the Book of Mormon confirm the divinity of Jesus Christ?

III. Purpose of Book of Mormon Today
   (Isa. 29:13-14, 4, 11-12 [K.J.]; Preface to B. of M.; II Nephi 2:19-23; Moroni 10:3-7; II Nephi 11:78)
   1. What do you think is the purpose of the Book of Mormon?
   2. Has the Book of Mormon helped you? How?
   3. What are some of the common misunderstandings about the book?
   4. How can you help more people understand the message of the Book of Mormon?

IV. Bible and Book of Mormon Harmony
   (Ezekiel 37:15-19; Mosiah 2:13-16; I Nephi 3:192-197; III Nephi 5:49-57; Mosiah 1:102-109)
   1. Does the Book of Mormon contradict the Bible at any point?
   2. Is it helpful to have another scripture to support the Bible?
   3. What would you think if a major doctrinal difference occurred in the Bible and Book of Mormon?
   4. What is the meaning of the biblical statement, "In the mouth of two or three witnesses shall every word be established"? (II Cor. 13:1)

V. New Light on the Living Christ
   (I Cor. 15:3-4, 14, 19-22; III Nephi 5:9-14; Ether 1:69-78; III Nephi 9:31-38; III Nephi 4:44-45, 50-52)
   1. Does the average Christian sense the reality of the living Christ?
   2. Do you feel the Book of Mormon information on Christ can serve a vital need today?
   3. What new light on the life and ministry of Jesus has the Book of Mormon given you?
   4. To what need in your life is Christ the answer?

174

VI. Faith in Christ Brings Confidence

(II Tim. 1:7; Heb. 10:35; I Nephi 1:65; I Nephi 5:59; Moroni 7:20)

1. Is self-confidence important to you?
2. How does faith in Christ help you to have self-confidence?
3. What area of daily life causes you to feel a need for more confidence and faith in Christ?
4. Do you sometimes think that following Christ would hurt your standing with people (temptation to trust in "arm of flesh")?
5. What is the difference between confidence in Christ and "cockiness"? Can you tell the difference?

VII. Signs Follow the Believer in Christ

(John 6:28-29; Mormon 4:85-88; Ether 1:107-109, 115; Mosiah 12:5-6; Mosiah 3:1-3)

1. Have you seen results of faith in anyone you know?
2. Why do you suppose God does not give "signs" to all people before they exercise faith?
3. What does faith in Christ mean in your daily life?
4. What "signs" do you desire to experience after the trial of your faith?
5. Why do some people want dramatic signs? Is this good?

VIII. Community Righteousness Results from Personal Response to Christ

(Matt. 6:31-33 [I.V. 6:35-38]; Nephi 3:187-188; Moroni 10:29; Ether 6:4, 8-10; IV Nephi 1:2-7, 13-14, 17-19; III Nephi 10:2-4)

1. Do you believe there will ever be a righteous community on earth?
2. Do individuals mold society, or does society mold the individuals?
3. Do you feel that a personal response to Jesus Christ by more individuals will help bring community righteousness? How?
4. How can the Book of Mormon help confront more persons with the living Christ?

Theme: GOSPEL PRINCIPLES

Topics

1. What is God like?

    Scriptures: Hebrews 11:1, 6; I John 4:7-11; Psalms 145:17-18; Amos 3:7; James 1:5-6

2. Who is Jesus?

    Scriptures: John 1:1-4, 10-2, 14; Matthew 1:18-23 (I.V. 2:1-6); Matthew 16:13-14 (I.V. 16:14-17); I Corinthians 15:14-22

3. What was Christ's message?

    Scriptures: John 3:3-8; Matthew 4:17-23 (I.V. 4:16-22); Hebrews 6:1-2; Matthew 26:26-29 (I.V. 22-26)

4. Is the Church of Jesus Christ essential or optional?

    Scriptures: Matthew 16:15-19 (I.V. 16-20); Acts 2:47; I Corinthians 12:12-14, 27-28; Colossians 1:16-18

5. What can we look forward to in the future of this world?

    Scriptures: Micah 4:1-4; Revelation 21:1-4; Matthew 24:3-7, 12-14, 29-31; (I.V. 24:4-6, 29-32, 37-40)

6. How can our faith be strengthened?

    Scriptures: Hebrews 11:1, 3, 5-8, 23-26, 29-30; Acts 26:16; Alma 16:149, 151-155, 158-166, 171-173

7. How can repentance affect our lives?

    Scriptures: Luke 24:46-47 (I.V. 45-46); II Corinthians 7:9-10; Isaiah 1:16-19; Acts 3:19

8. What can new birth mean in our lives?

    Scriptures: John 3:3-5; John 10:1-5; Romans 6:3-13; Acts 8:14-17

Theme

BELIEFS THAT MATTER IN THE BATTLE OF LIFE

Topics

1. The Human-Divine Encounter

    Scriptures: (King James Version) Heb. 11:1-3, 6; John 17:1-3; I John 4:13-15; D. and C. 17:4a-c

2. When God Visited the Planet

    Scriptures: Matt. 1:23; John 1:14; John 14:6-11; B. of M. 251:28-32

176

3. Revelation-Relevant Religion

   Scriptures: Matt. 16:16-17; Amos 3:7; Gal. 1:11-12; Rev. 19:10; I Cor. 14:1

4. Christ's Commissioned Church

   Scriptures: Matt. 16:16-19; Eph. 4:11-14; Eph. 5:23-24; I Cor. 12:27-28

5. The Scriptures Light the Path

   Scriptures: II Tim. 3:14-17; Acts 17:11; I Peter 1:24-25; Isaiah 29:11-14; Alma 12:4-5

6. Principles of the Joyous Life

   Scriptures: Ps. 1:1-2; Heb. 6:1-2; Matt. 17:19-20; Eph. 6:16; Acts 2:38

7. When the Community Is Converted

   Scriptures: Matt. 6:31-33; Rev. 21:1-4; Ps. 50:2-5; Micah 4:1-5

Theme

COMING OF CHRIST BRINGS MEANING TO LIFE

Topics

I. Significance of the Coming of Christ
   (Do we really know who Jesus is?)
      (Isa. 9:6; Matt. 1:23 [I.V. 2:6]; John 1:3-5, 10-14; John 14:6-11)

   1. Is Jesus God?
   2. Was Jesus human like other men?
   3. Can we know Jesus today as much as he was known when he was on earth?
   4. Did Jesus know everything at birth, or did he have to learn like other men?
   5. Did Jesus ever sin?
   6. How can we get to know the man, Jesus, personally today?

II. Meaning of Life Revealed in Christ
   (Do we really know his purpose?)
      (John 3:13-19; II Cor. 5:17-19; Isa. 53:4-7, 12; Phil. 2:5-7, 3:7-10; I John 4:7-11)

   1. What was the main mission of Christ?
   2. Did Jesus have to die?

3. What did his death and resurrection accomplish?
4. How is the meaning of life revealed in Christ to us?
5. How did Jesus demonstrate the love of God?
6. How did Christ reveal the purpose of man?

III. Courageous Commitment to Christ
(Have we made a serious commitment to Christ?)
(Matt. 22:36-40 [I.V. 35-39]; Mark 8:34-38 [I.V. 36-41];
Matt. 11:28-30 [I.V. 29-30]; Matt. 19:27-30)
1. Did Jesus ask his followers primarily for a pledge of deep
loyalty or obedience to a strict moral code?
2. What is the nature of the commitment Jesus asks us to make?
3. How did he tell us to show our willingness to make a
commitment?
4. What ordinance of the church is the beginning of our act of
commitment to Christ?
5. Does our level of commitment grow or is it a "once and for
all-time step"?

IV. Making Christ Lord of Daily Life
(Can we relate our commitment to daily life where money and
possessions are involved?)
(Matt. 19:16-23; Matt. 6:19-21; Matt. 6:24-33; Malachi
3:7-10)
1. What is the attitude Christ wants us to have toward physical
possessions?
2. Why do we sometimes feel that accumulation of wealth and
material possessions will bring security and happiness? Does it?
3. Are material things evil?
4. What is tithing?
5. How can we rob God?
6. Can the Christian use of material things help to strengthen our
spiritual life?

V. Strength in Christ to Forsake Pride and Strife
(Can we relate the experience of Christ in our life to the daily
temptations of pride . . . desire for praise and power . . . urge to
control others?)
(Matt. 18:1-4 [I.V. 1-3]; Matt. 23:5-10 [I.V. 4-9]; Prov.
28:25; James 4:10, 5:16; I John 2:16)

178

1. Was Jesus faced with these temptations? (Matt. 4:1-10)
2. What did Jesus mean about men becoming as little children?
3. What is humility?
4. Why is pride so destructive to the spiritual life of a disciple?
5. Are people today becoming more loving and kind or more hateful and indifferent?
6. What can we do to forsake our pride and become more openly honest and transparently real?
7. How important is it to act "natural"? Are there times when it is difficult to be our real selves?

VI. Power in Christ to Bear Effective Witness
(Can we relate our experience of Christ to someone else in a significant way?)
   (Matt. 28:18-20 [I.V. 17-19]; Acts 1:8; James 5:19-20; Prov. 11:30)
1. Does Christ expect all his followers to witness?
2. Why are we reluctant to testify to others?
3. What is a testimony?
4. How can we improve in our ability to get across to others what we have felt?
5. How important is outreach?

VII. Entering into the Kingdom of Love and Life
(Can we surrender our will gladly to God and enter his kingdom way provided in the latter days?)
   (John 3:3-5; Matt. 4:17, 23 [I.V. 16:22]; Matt. 5:3-10 [I.V. 5-12]; John 14:15, 21, 23; John 13:34-35; John 10:10)
1. What does it mean to be born again?
2. What is surrender to Christ?
3. Do we feel it is a happy experience to obey God's will against our own?
4. What does Weatherhead mean by saying the kingdom of God is the kingdom of happy relationships?
5. Is there a need to be baptized in the church of Jesus Christ Restored (Christ's body) to enter the kingdom?
6. Can we have our membership in the church and not be in Christ's kingdom?
7. How can we help Christ build up his kingdom on earth?

Theme: *CHRIST'S KINGDOM IS COMING*

Topics

1. Does Christ's kingdom exist now?
   - *1. Matt. 4:17   *Matt. 3:28
   - 2. Matt. 10:7   Matt. 7:9
   - 3. Luke 17:20-21   Luke 17:20-21
   - 4.   none   Genesis 9:22-23

2. Shall Christ's kingdom come on earth?
   - 1. Matt. 6:9-10   Matt. 6:10-11
   - 2. Rev. 21:1-4   Rev. 21:1-4
   - 3. Micah 4:1-2   Micah 4:1-2
   - 4. Matt. 24:3, 14   Matt. 24:4, 32

3. What are the characteristics of Christ's kingdom?
   - 1. John 14:1-6   John 14:1-6
   - 2. John 1:10-14   John 1:10-14
   - 3. I John 3:1-2   I John 3:1-2
   - 4. Matt. 5:3-10   Matt. 5:4-12

4. Is Christ's church essential to bring forth his kingdom?
   - 1. Rev. 12:5, 17   Rev. 12:2, 3, 7, 17
   - 2. Matt. 16:18-19   Matt. 16:19-20
   - 3. Eph. 4:11-15   Eph. 4:11-15
   - 4. Eph. 5:23-24, 30-32   Eph. 5:23-24, 30-32

5. Are ordinances essential to help persons into Christ's kingdom?
   - 1. John 3:3-5   John 3:3-5
   - 2. Mark 16:16   Mark 16:16
   - 3. Acts 2:38   Acts 2:38
   - 4. John 6:51-52   John 6:51-52

6. Do some ministers have more authority from God to guide men toward his kingdom?
   - 1. John 15:16   John 15:16
   - 2. Matt. 18:17-18   Matt. 18:17-18
   - 3. Acts 8:9-10, 14-23   Acts 8:9-10, 14-23
   - 4. Heb. 5:4 (Ex. 28:1)   Heb. 5:4 (Ex. 28:1)

---

*First column references, King James; second column, Inspired Version.

7. Are the gifts of the Holy Spirit presently guiding in the kingdom endeavor?

1. I Cor. 12:1, 8-10	I Cor. 12:1, 7-11
2. James 5:14-15	James 5:14-15
3. I Cor. 14:1, 22, 39	I Cor. 14:1, 22, 39
4. Rev. 19:10	Rev. 19:10
5. I John 4:1-3	I John 4:1-3

8. How can we enter the kingdom now?

1. Matt. 7:21	Matt. 7:30
2. Matt. 10:38-39	Matt. 10:33-34
3. II Nephi 13:24	
4. Moroni 8:29	
5. Moroni 6:2-6	

ADDITIONAL DISCUSSION TOPICS

Theme: *"CHRIST IS CALLING US"*
The Sound of His Voice

Personal preparation is essential to attune ourselves to the revelation of Christ. What that experience means in individual lives is very important. The process of discovering our relationship with the living Christ can become the most meaningful adventure in life. What preparation is necessary to hear his call?

1. Matt. 5:3-11
2. John 3:16
3. John 17:11

He Calls Us to Himself

As we study the life of our Lord we can identify with him. The life and ministry of Christ is the central issue in life. Christians have Christ as the center (hero) of their lives. How does he call persons today? Is Christ God, man, or both? Does it matter?

> 1. Matt. 11:28
> 2. Matt. 19:17
> 3. Mark 8:34-35

He Calls Us to Wholeness

Repentance precedes conversion. We become new persons as we identify with the Lord Jesus. We see ourselves through his vision and the potential which is within us. We can develop wholesome selfhood. How does Christ make men whole? What is repentance? Conversion? Must we sense our need for help before we move toward Christ?

> 1. Matt. 5:48
> 2. II Cor. 17-19
> 3. Col. 1:25-27

He Calls Us to Religious Experience

Conversion is a process. The religious experiences of great men help explain the revelatory process. As we identify with these experiences we see how they can be relevant and productive in our times. What was Joseph Smith's experience? Can this happen now?

> 1. James 1:5
> 2. Rev. 14:6-7
> 3. Zech. 2:3-4

He Calls Us to Search and Share

We need to search the scriptures. We have Three Standard Books. We need to extend our search to all good books. Do the scriptures all agree? Why have the Book of Mormon? The Doctrine and Covenants? What is the best way to read the scriptures? (John 5:39; Acts 2:41-42; Isaiah 29:4; 11-14; 17-18)

He Calls Us to Relatedness

As we mature in our fellowship with him we expand our thinking so we more easily recognize the need to relate all of our religious experience to an eternal structure. This doesn't begin in the hereafter; it begins here and now and continues in the hereafter. We see the whole person as Paul saw the church "with members in particular," working together; as we relate to each other in a common task of service and ministry we are led to real brotherhood. Life is relationship (Matt. 6:19-21; II Cor. 5:1; John 4:13-14).

He Calls Us to Brotherhood

The mission of the church is Zion, the expression of the universal kingdom. Stewardship—both on a personal and social level—will bring about Zion. As we dream of Zion we also need to see the practical and basic ways people today can help bring Zion forth (Matt. 25:35-40; Isa. 2:1-4; Matt. 24:14).

He Calls Us to Be on the Growing Edge

We have come this far only because those who preceded us were on the growing edge. They left us a heritage which we must extend and pass on to our youth. We are called to be people of vision who will not only dream but dare the "impossible." We need to say, "I can do all things through Christ who strengtheneth me." We are called to faith, to unity, to exploring outreach, and to daring adventure (Matt. 7:7-11; II Tim. 1:7; Phil. 4:13).

Discussion Notes

1. Questions should be carefully formulated ahead of each discussion meeting. They should be "open-ended" with more than a "yes" or "no" answer.

2. The objectives of the discussions are to (a) prepare for

worship, (b) move closer to each other in saintly love and understanding, (c) stimulate desire for more understanding, (d) interest everyone in a deeper involvement with Christ.

3. Sharing feelings is far more important than trying to change someone. There should be no attempt to convince, preach, or exhort in this particular setting.

4. The thing that is sought is a group atmosphere of loving acceptance where each can *feel* the gospel of God's great love as he explores his own understanding. Prayer—not argument—is the key to success.

OTHER SMALL GROUP DISCUSSIONS

1. What are the characteristics of Christ's kingdom?
   —a weekly study of the beatitudes and other scripture relating to the kingdom.
2. What is Jesus like?
   —a probe into the scriptures revealing certain aspects of his personality
   —a study on how he dealt with various problems of life which we face today
3. Is God at work in the world today?
   —a study of the Restoration movement with an emphasis on God's present tense activity in the world.
4. What is the nature, function, and mission of the Church?
   —an examination of those scriptures throwing light on what Christ thought about the church.
5. What are the principles of life?
   —a weekly discussion of the basic six principles of the gospel and how they relate to our life today
6. What is the purpose of priesthood in our day?
   —a scriptural examination of authority and its purpose in ministry

7. What is Zion and how can we help bring it today?

—a study on the nature of the kingdom and those processes essential to bring it about.

8. What is the relation of the Holy Scriptures to the principle of revelation?

—an examination of the three books and their purpose in light of our belief in "revelation."

—a discussion on what is revelation and how it works with individuals as well as with the organized church through the prophet.

9. What was the basic message of Jesus?

—a probe into those scriptures which reveal the core of his preaching and teaching, making application to our needs today.

10. How does one become effective in winning others to Christ?

—a discussion on the essentials of personal witnessing.

11. How does one cultivate his prayer life?

—a scriptural study of prayer, its need in our lives, purpose.

12. How would an ideal "steward" feel and act in today's world?

13. What kind of family life is essential for Zion?

14. What is eternal life?

BIBLE CELL MEDITATION
How to Develop Discussion on Scripture

What is the main truth of this verse?
What other scripture can I find to illuminate this verse?
(Look up the margin references given in the Bible)
Is there any word or part of this verse which I do not understand?

Is there a command, or word of advice, here to obey?
Is there a good example to follow?
Is there a sin or mistake to avoid?
Is there a warning to heed?
Is there a promise to claim?
Is there a prayer to echo?
How can I see my own experience reflected here?
How can I apply this scripture to practical, everyday life?
How can I turn this verse into a prayer?

After you have had a period of silent prayer and meditation, ask the group to tell just what God has said to each person. After that, take the second verse in a similar manner, and so on.

Copies of this Bible Meditation Card can be obtained, price 25c per dozen (postage and packing extra), from the Bookroom, Hildenborough Hall, Otford Hills, Sevenoaks, Kent, England.

Bibliography

1. Casteel, John L., ed., *Spiritual Renewal Through Personal Groups,* Association Press, New York, 1957.

2. Coleman, Lyman, *Growth by Groups,* Christian Outreach, Huntingdom Valley, Pennsylvania.

3. *Creating Christian Cells,* Pamphlet by Faith at Work, Columbia, Maryland.

4. Drakeford, John W., *Integrity Therapy,* Broadman Press, Nashville, 1967.

5. *Faith at Work Magazine,* published by Word, Inc., Waco, Texas.

6. *Fellowship Evangelism Through Church Groups,* Bethany Press, St. Louis, 1951.

7. Freer and Hall, *Two or Three Together,* Harpers, New York, 1954.

8. Miller, Paul M., *Group Dynamics in Evangelism,* Harold Press, Scottsdale, Pennsylvania, 1958.

9. Howe, Reuel, *The Miracle of Dialogue,* Seabury Press, New York, 1963.

10. Howe, Reuel, *Man's Need and God's Action,* Seabury Press, Greenwich, Connecticut.

11. Lacour, Lawrence L., *How to Conduct a Discussion Group,* Tidings Press, Nashville, Tennessee.

12. Leslie, Robert C., *Sharing Groups in the Church,* Abingdon Press, Nashville, 1971.

13. Miller, Keith, *Taste of New Wine,* Word Books, Waco, Texas, 1965.

14. Cartwright, Dorwin, and Zader, Alvin, *Group Dynamics,* Harper and Row, New York 1968.

15. Casteel, John, *The Creative Role of Interpersonal Groups in the Church Today*, Association Press, New York, 1968.

16. Rogers, Carl, *On Becoming a Person*, Houghton Mifflin Company, Boston, 1965.

17. Rogers, Carl, *Client-Centered Therapy*, Houghton Mifflin Company, 1965

18. Shoemaker, Samuel, *The Experiment of Faith*, Harper Brothers, New York, 1958.

19. Shoemaker, Samuel, *How to Become a Christian*, Harper Brothers, New York, 1957

20. Shoemaker, Samuel, *Beginning Your Ministry*, Harper Brothers, New York, 1963.

21. Shoemaker, Samuel, *With Holy Spirit and Fire*, Harper Brothers, New York, 1960.

22. Shoemaker, Samuel, "The Church and Awakening Groups" (article in October 10, 1960, *Christianity Today*).

23. Webber, George, *God's Colony in Man's World*, Abingdon Press, Nashville, 1960.

24. Jourard, Sidney M., *The Transparent Self*, Van Nostrand Co., Inc., 1964.

25. Kerlinger, Fred, *Foundations of Behavioral Research*, Holt, Rinehart, and Winston, New York, 1964.

26. Olmsted, Michael S., *The Small Group*, Random House, New York, 1959.

27. Osborn, Cecil, *The Art of Understanding Yourself*, Zondervan Books, Grand Rapids, Michigan, 1967.

28. Miles, Matthew B., *Learning to Work in Groups*, College Press, Columbia University, New York, 1965.

29. Rogers, Carl, "Process of the Basic Encounter Group," Western Behavioral Science Institute, La Jolla California, (1967 article).

30. Rogers, Carl, "U.S.A. 2000" symposium presentation at San Francisco, January 10, 1968.

Suggested Reading

Casteel, John L., *The Creative Role of Interpersonal Groups in the Church Today*, New York, Association Press, $4.95. (A ten-years-later look at groups in the church by Casteel and fifteen specialists who are aware of new understandings of group experience.)

Coleman, Lyman, *Groups in Action*, Halfway House, Newtown, Pennsylvania, 1968. (A beautifully put together booklet with pictures describing how a group moves into action. The insert provides groups with a structured workbook, enabling them to move toward an expression of mission.)

Day, Leroy Judson, *Dynamic Christian Fellowship,* Judson Press, Valley Forge, 1968, revised edition, $1.50. (A book which covers a wide range of small group expressions in the church.)

Deshler, G. Byron, *The Power of the Personal Group,* Tidings, Nashville, 65c. (An explanation of what really happens in the personal group. Group dynamics are traced in easily readable form.)

Emerick, Samuel, *A Manual for Prayer Groups,* The Upper Room, Nashville, 1958. (Practical helps for group leaders and pastors.)

Leslie, Robert C., *Sharing Groups,* Abingdon Press, Nashville, 1971. (An excellent paperback for leaders.)

Little, Sara, *Learning Together in the Christian Fellowship,* Richmond, John Knox Press, 1956, 25c. (A practical study of group dynamics and their application to Christian fellowship.)

Mowrer, O. Hobart, *The New Group Therapy*, Princeton, Van Nostrand, 1964, $2.45. (A look at group life in the secular field of psychology with consideration given to "openness to others.")

Reid, Clyde, *Groups Alive—Church Alive*, New York, Harper & Row, 1969, $3.95. (A new basic handbook outlining crucial elements of group life. From his wealth of insight and experience, Reid writes on purpose, leadership, disciplines, size, atmosphere, phases, the individual, problems, and nonverbal methods.)

Rinker, Rosalind, *Prayer—Conversing with God*, Zondervan, Grand Rapids, 1959, $1.00. (An introduction to conversational prayer. Helpful for groups.)

Rinker, Rosalind, *Praying Together*, Zondervan, Grand Rapids, 1968, $2.95. (A recent application of conversational prayer to the small group. A good basic book for people who are just getting started in attempts to pray together.)

Raines, Robert, *New Life in the Church*, Harper & Row, New York, 1961, $3.00. (A standard for churches interested in renewal via small groups; a report of renewal in the Aldersgate Methodist Church in Cleveland.)

Groups That Work, Grand Rapids, Zondervan, 1967, $1.95. (A collection of chapters by various authors on what groups can be and what they can do. Bruce Larson, Keith Miller, Rosalind Rinker, Sam Shoemaker, Robert Raines, and Gordon Cosby are the contributors.)

Pastoral Psychology, Vol. 15, No. 145, June 1964; Vol. 18, No. 172, March 1967; Manhasset, New York. (These two issues were devoted to the subject of small groups and their role in the church.)